HARD
AS
NAILS

To John Chessire – without such men the First World War would not have been won and Britain would never have been great.

HARD AS NAILS

THE SPORTSMEN'S BATTALION OF WORLD WAR ONE

MICHAEL FOLEY

SPELLMOUNT

www.authorsites.co.uk/michaelfoley

British Library Cataloguing in Publication Data:
A catalogue record for this book is available
from the British Library

Copyright © Michael Foley 2007

ISBN 978 186227 406 8

First published in the UK in 2007 by
Spellmount Limited
The Mill, Brimscombe Port
Stroud, Gloucestershire. GL5 2QG

Tel: 01453 883300
Fax: 01453 883233
E-mail: enquiries@spellmount.com
Website: www.spellmount.com

1 3 5 7 9 8 6 4 2

Printed in Great Britain by
Oaklands Book Services
Stonehouse, Gloucestershire GL10 3RQ

CONTENTS

ACKNOWLEDGEMENTS

I would like to express my thanks to C. Chaloner for the permission to use her illustrations. I would also like to thank her for allowing me to read and use other material relating to her grandfather John Chessire, of the 1st Sportsmen's Battalion.

All other illustrations are from my private collection. Although every attempt has been made to find the copyright owner of all the illustrations, I offer my unreserved apologies to anyone whose copyright has been unintentionally breached and request they contact me through the publisher.

INTRODUCTION

The First World War was unique for many reasons, not least because it was the first time that Britain had assembled such a large army. The British Army, distinctive in being initially volunteer based, rapidly developed into a conscripted force. Up until this war, Britain had always had small professional forces. This new Army was singular in the way that large numbers of its recruits were grouped into units, many of which represented a specific geographical area, such as the Pals Battalions, consisting of men from the same town or village. Heavy casualties within a unit meant the near complete decimation of the young male population from many British towns and villages.

Other units grouped men of similar talents, such as the Artist Rifles; this unit was not instigated for the war but had origins in the rifle volunteers of the nineteenth century. The almost total destruction of the Artist Rifles early in the war led to the deaths of many talented young men. It also led to their reassignment as an officer training battalion, in which some of the famous war poets, such as Wilfred Owen and Edward Thomas, served, but subsequently met their deaths in the regiments they had moved into as trained officers.

There were other special battalions raised, such as the University and Public Schools Battalion (UPS), which was a sort of an up-market Pals Battalion. Units such as these had serious flaws in that most of the men who enlisted in the ranks were seen as 'officer class', and so many of them were commissioned that the very make-up of the battalions developed into an entirely different proposition than had originally been envisaged. This was what happened to most of the specialised battalions, as replacements for those who had fallen or been commissioned came from all walks of life.

Then came the unit that is the subject of this book: The Sportsmen's Battalion. Raised by Mrs Cunliffe Owen, the battalion was quickly given the nickname, 'Hard as Nails Corps', due to the fine physique of its recruits, mostly men renowned in the worlds of sport or entertainment. They were men used to the active outdoor life and made impressive-looking soldiers. Many of them stood over 6ft tall, much above the average male height at that time. They also suffered from the problem of losing a good number of men to commissions, as many of them came from the class of men perceived as 'good officer material'.

In the trenches of France, it was debatable how much difference the physique of each soldier made. When German machine-guns swept British troops advancing across No Man's Land, the strong fell along with the weak, as did ex-public schoolboys and labourers.

The Sportsmen's Battalion was, however, a unique development in a terrible conflict. The notion that wars were won on the playing fields of public schools was carried to its extreme in their formation. Another view was that battles were won by those who were 'thrusters' at the upper-class sport of foxhunting. There is little doubt that the courage required for the cavalry officers of Wellington's Army was developed during pre-war hunting while jumping a thousand fences. Siegfried Sassoon's *Memoirs of a Foxhunting Man* makes it clear that this theory could be applied to the First World War, although the days of the cavalry were numbered once the machine-guns began to fire.

Another exclusive development for the Sportsmen's Battalion was their special dispensation to enlist men up to forty-five years of age. Their superior fitness meant they were so fit they were still able to fight, despite their advanced age. Although this higher age limit has been widely publicised, what is less well known is that most of the men over forty years were removed from service on the front line after a very short period. There were similarly a number of older men left kicking their heels in England when the battalion moved overseas.

Although the battalion was made up of men from the highest and most loyal ranks of society, there was at one point a suspicion, again not widely known, that one of its members may have been a traitor who gave away secrets of a British attack on the enemy.

John Chessire's family in the late nineteenth century. Back row, left to right: Maud, John Reginald, Cecil, Cyril. Front: Ada, John Stanley, Muriel. (C. Chaloner)

Generally, the soldiers of the special battalions who enlisted for service in the war did so without much thought to the consequences. Although successful in encouraging enlistment, the battalions suffered from several problems once they were raised; despite this, the men cannot be criticised for their bravery or patriotism. As with most such difficulties during the First World War, the fault seemed to lie with those in command and not the common soldier, who, despite terrible conditions, tended to get on with the job while maintaining a cheerful nature.

Although much of the information in this book comes from written sources, such as the publications from the period, there are also eyewitness accounts of the battalion's existence from its formation, well into the conflict and after the armistice. This information comes mainly from the letters of John Keeble Claughton Chessire, who was a member of the battalion from its early formation at the Hotel Cecil. Unfortunately for us, he was one of those men over the age of forty who was soon removed from front line action, and so we have lost an intelligent commentary on the later years of the war from this perspective. Of course, it was not an unfortunate turn of events for him. However, from reading his letters, I feel I know enough about him to be confident about his strong sense of duty and realise he was unlikely to have been happy about losing his place at the front. His letters give a great insight into the feelings of the men involved in the war.

Thankfully, for those of us interested in the history of the First World War, Private Chessire was a great letter writer and talented artist. Thanks to his family, who preserved these letters and other items from his service, we can learn a little more about how it must have been to serve in one of the most horrific wars that has ever been. What is certain is that despite problems with the organisation of the Army, the Sportsmen's Battalion gave a great account of itself throughout the war.

SOMEWHERE IN FRANCE

By John Chessire

Near to the place there was a garden where many soldiers were sleeping.
Each with a little white cross at his head.
And towards evening the shadows of these little crosses would creep silently
over the beds in which they were sleeping.
Until they were all lost in the twilight.

Sleep warriors sleep.
While the sun falls asleep.
The shadow of thy little crosses will creep.
Into the twilight.
While you sleep.

Dream warrior dream
Thy life was all a dream
Dream till the shadow of thy cross will seem.
The loveliest thing in all thy dream.

'Somewhere in France' was written by John Chessire during the war. The poem illustrates the sadness of so many lives lost in the conflict. I do not think it was a protest against the war, unlike the anti-war feeling demonstrated by many of the war poets – not everyone who fought in the war felt its futility. Some men, like John Chessire, went through the war believing strongly in the justification of the British position and the need for the war. Charles Sorley said of poets like Rupert Brooke that they were far too obsessed with their own sacrifice in going to war, when standing up to fight was really just what was expected of them and every other man. John Chessire was a typical example of the kind of man who fought in the Sportsmen's Battalion, and in many other units. A gentleman who believed in fair play and the British way of life, he did not make a fuss about fulfilling his responsibilities even in the worst conditions. He believed that it was his sincere duty.

There were times when the duties of war Chessire was obligated to undertake would have been firmly at odds with his beliefs. Some of his comments on religion suggest he would have suffered great dismay at the thought of taking a life. In one letter, he comments that the ideal soldier would not be religious. There may have been even times when he was unsure about the patriotism that was displayed at home, but this seemed to be more to do with his not wanting to rejoice in the horror of war. Like many English gentlemen, he wanted to do the job modestly and quickly and then go home to his family, leaving aside the flag-waving jingoism of those at home who knew nothing of what war was really about.

John came from a background that would likely be described as the lower gentry. His father was a vicar at Hindlip, in Worcestershire. At the turn of the century, clergymen were relatively well paid and often the younger children of well-off families. John was the third of seven children. His sister, Maud, who was the second child, wrote of the family that they were a most happy and united group. Until their mother died, when Maud was seventeen, she had never known or experienced any real sorrow. She described her mother as always anxious to fill the children's minds with only beautiful thoughts and she was obviously very successful at this.

Maud described her father as a man of sterling qualities, straight as a die, very reserved and of great intellectual and spiritual charm as well as being artistic and sensitive. I believe that John resembled his father in most of those characteristics, except perhaps one: Maud described her father as being too tender for the real world, a man who could not have faced it at all if not for the support of her mother. John seems to have inherited many of his father's characteristics but nonetheless had the ability to face the world without qualms. His sense of duty shone through his actions in all he did, and he never seemed to display any hint of fear in what must have been some very trying and, at times, terrifying situations.

John sent many skilful paintings home from the service in France, indicative of his education at the Slade School of Art. These paintings were often painted on old cigarette packets or from whatever materials were available. He had a very good education, and had published a book before the war called the *Bethlehem Tableaux*, a religious do-it-yourself manual for schools and churches. Religion was always important to him but he never pursued it as far as his brother Reginald, who became the vicar of Wribbenhall, where John lived and his children were born after he married Dorothy in 1903.

John was responsible for producing an historical pageant at Hartelbury Castle. History was another of his great interests. He had put on a beautiful production of his *Bethlehem Tableaux* in the diocese, which was subsequently reported in the *Church Times* and the *Worcester Herald*.

Before the war, John worked for his brother-in-law, the Honourable Percy Allsop, in the Allsop family's brewing business. Percy was married to John's sister, Maud. The brewery went broke in 1913, mainly due to the attempt to bring lager to Britain. The brewery was ahead of its time. Because of John's family connection, he resigned when the business was taken over.

John had a keen sense of humour; he wrote a long and witty poem about the demise of the brewery called, 'Allsops In Wonderland'. Below are the first three verses (the complete version has fifteen):

> *The board were sitting after tea.*
> *And far into the night.*
> *Trying their level best to keep.*
> *Shareholders smooth and bright.*
> *And this was difficult because.*
> *It was such an uphill fight*
>
> *The board were sitting sulkily.*
> *Because of banner one.*
> *Who had no business to be there.*
> *After the day was done.*
> *It is very rude of him they said.*
> *To come and spoil the fun.*

John in 1912 with his daughters, who he missed greatly while serving in the Sportsmen's Battalion. Back row, left to right: Betty, Frances; front row: Anne, John, Deborah. (C. Chaloner)

The board of all directors.
The shrewdest in the land.
Did weep like anything to see.
So many notes of hand.
If these were only cleared away.
They said it would be grand.

John was not employed when the war began but seemed to have had an income from somewhere, as by then he had four children. His wife Dorothy had a further private income from her father, which ended when he died causing the family financial problems during the war.

The Sportsmen's Battalion may have seemed a strange choice for John, although he did have a great interest in golf; but there was another, principal, reason for his choosing the Sportsmen. When the war began, at forty-three years of age, John was too old to enlist with any other unit, and being very tall, he fitted into this regiment rather well.

After the war, John did not seem to have employment. His family believes that the war affected him and afterwards he was never the same man. This may have been a result of his being gassed or may have had a less physical cause. Still, although not visibly employed, John must have had some income as his daughters attended boarding school. He died in 1934 from pneumonia.

The original plan was that this book would be solely about the Sportsmen's Battalion, and John Chessire's role within it, but it became apparent that it was impossible to do this without taking account of other units, and the war in general. No battalion fought on their own; each was part of a larger unit of a brigade, and each brigade part of a division.

CHAPTER I

RECRUITING FOR THE WAR

Although war had been threatening for years in Europe, when it came the conflict was sudden and widespread. The plans and hopes of many of the European states were in disacord, a situation echoed across other parts of the world. The move from peace to war was dramatic after the assassination of Archduke Ferdinand, the spark that lit the fire.

Britain had only a small-standing Army at the time. When one considers the size of the pre-war Empire, it is amazing that the Army numbered less than half a million at the outbreak of war, and enlarging the forces was the first major task for the country. This was to be the first war that was fought by a civilian army. Until this time, the professional soldiers of a modest army had always been strong enough to deal with small-scale wars and local conflicts that preceded the First World War.

Despite the impending threat of war, there had been little preparation for it in Britain. *The Great War* magazine reported that despite the terrible lessons of the South African conflict, and the numerous political committees and commissions advising reform, the outbreak of war still found Britain trying to maintain the largest Empire in the world with an Army insufficient in size for a third-class military power.

The beginning of the war saw an Army still run based on the experience of the wars of the previous century. On the third day of mobilisation, an order went out that all officers were to have their swords sharpened. When the attacks began from the trenches, officers were more likely to disguise themselves as other ranks to prevent enemy snipers picking off officers first. Carrying a sword would have been as good as offering themselves up as targets. The French Army was larger than the British, but still poorly adapted for the modern war that was to come. The French were still wearing red kepis and red trousers – clearly visible to German machine-gunners.

The men of the regular Army who were the first to arrive in France had little experience of dealing with members of the new Army. Any information they did get came mainly from the staff and commanding officers of the new Army units, who were sent to France for a short time to experience life in the line before their men were sent abroad.

Lord Kitchener was appointed as secretary of war in August 1914. Although many thought that the war would end quickly, Kitchener did not. He believed that the war would be very costly in lives and that it would be won by the last million men that Britain could send into battle. This was not a point of view supported by many politicians.

Kitchener's first task was to persuade men to join the Army. Conscription was not acceptable to the country at the time, despite it being the norm in most other countries involved in the conflict. Over 10,000 men enlisted over the weekend of 18 August 1914. This was a good start, but the target Kitchener had set was 100,000 men between the ages of nineteen and thirty, with chest sizes of at least 34in and reaching a height of at least 5ft 3in. This was to be the first 100,000. By the end of the month, another 100,000 men were needed and the upper age limit was then raised to thirty-five.

The recruiting figures for London alone for the ten days at the end of August and early September were published in *The Times*:

August	26	1,725	September	1	4,600
	27	1,650		2	4,500
	28	1,780		3	3,600
	29	1,800		4	4,028
	30	1,928			
	31	1,620			

Kitchener visited 17,000 of the new recruits at Shorncliffe Camp in Kent. Discipline was very quickly instilled. When ordered to advance at double speed, the recruits did just that and Lord Kitchener had to move out of the way very smartly before he was trampled.

Winston Churchill did his best to help recruitment and attached a placard to the back of his car to encourage men to enlist. The

Posters were not required for some men, as this crowd besieging the recruiting office in Whitehall shows.

promotion of patriotic fervour was pursued by every means. There were widespread stories of German atrocities committed against the people of Belgium. Patriotic poems were published in *The Times* by writers such as Rudyard Kipling, who donated his £50 fee to the Belgian Relief Fund, and Thomas Hardy, who did not claim copyright for his poem.

Many private companies actually encouraged their workers to enlist, which seems a very selfless act when one considers that they would be losing their work force. Despite this, many offered financial incentives, such as a £2 bonus for young single male employees who joined up. Others offered regular amounts, ranging from 5s to half their normal wages every week while they served. Some railway companies treated men who joined up as though they were on leave and continued to pay a full wage. Civil servants who were called up to be reservists or territorials were to carry on receiving their civil service pay.

Along with the patriotism came rumours that pointed to less positive forces operating from within the country. A letter written to the

Westminster Gazette from someone complaining about the casualties in Belgium was reported as being from a fictitious person and address. The ink used to write the letter was a shade of color rarely seen in England. There were early attempts to discredit any criticism of the war effort.

In *The Times* of 28 August 1914 a letter was published stating that for every man who enlisted, there were ten who had not. These men were described as laggards who should feel ashamed. The letter went on to point out that every regiment had a depot where recruits were welcome and every territorial battalion had a recruiting officer.

There were regularly updated maps of the front lines printed in *The Times*, which made available what would have appeared to be sensitive information. There did not seem to be any Government plan for propaganda in the press at the beginning of the war. There was a feeling that everyone should get behind the war effort, and those who ran the newspapers tried to promote this in the manner they thought best. Kitchener was in many ways hostile towards the press but needed it to help with his recruitment drive. Many of the comics or newspapers for young people were also run by the men who owned the daily newspapers. These comics had long promoted an image of the patriotic brave young man who did his bit for the country. Most of these comic book heroes were young men from a public school background. There were those who believed that the tone of these comics was an attempt to pass values of the public schoolboy onto the working-class youngsters who read them – a useful method of influence in a country hungry for patriotic young men.

Initially, the national press was mainly self-regulating but supported the aims of the war and so presented no problem to the Government. The local press was initially left alone as well but this policy led to problems. There were often examples of more critical letters from the front being published locally because the national press would not print them.

Direct Government control was needed, and eventually the Official Secrets Act was passed along with the Defence of the Realm Act (DORA). By 1915 the press was allowed at the front but was controlled and censored by the Army. By the end of the war, those who owned the press had obtained powerful positions in the control of war news. Lord Northcliffe, who owned the *Mail* and *The Times*, was by then the Director of Propaganda in Enemy Countries.

RALLY ROUND THE FLAG

EVERY FIT MAN WANTED

One of the numerous recruiting posters intended to encourage men to enlist.

Raising an army, with press backing, was going very well. In fact, so many men enlisted that the Army and its War Office could not cope with the huge numbers. There were not enough khaki uniforms to go round, so many wore blue uniforms. There was also a shortage of weapons. This failure of the War Office was one reason why many battalions were raised by private men and women who supplied and trained men until the War Office was able to take over these units. In many cases, the money needed to pay for battalions' equipment was raised amongst the more well-to-do recruits or by the rich men who formed the units.

Recruits came not only from Britain but from other parts of the Empire. There were another 80,000 men from Canada, to add to the 20,000 already being equipped. There were 60,000 US citizens who had offered to enlist in the Canadian Army, as well as 100,000 promised from India. A corps of 'Rough Riders' was formed in Canada, the applicants being expert horsemen and good shots. Many of them were American cowboys. The 1,000-strong Loyal Edmonton Regiment was raised in Canada in only eight days, and also included a company of Sportsmen.

Lloyd George even attempted to raise a Welsh army corps of 50,000 men. He said that most Welshmen would love to see a Welsh army in the field. However, there were disagreements between Lloyd George and Kitchener over this plan. The hope that only the Welsh language was to be spoken on parade was a non-starter and Kitchener was against the army being used for political gain. There were never enough recruits for Lloyd George's grand plan anyway and instead of a corps, the final result was a Welsh division. In October, there was a report in *The Times* by a correspondent who witnessed the training of one of the battalions of the Welsh Division. The correspondent was in the Rhondda Valley watching a miners' battalion on a route march. He described the men as undersized in height but broad of shoulder and strong. He had no doubt that they would make fine soldiers.

There were several attempts to raise the number of men joining the Army from other sources. Territorial battalions were invited to volunteer to serve overseas, with seventy such battalions coming forward. The idea that men would be willing to serve with others whom they knew came from Sir Henry Rawlinson. Recruitment campaigns were started in towns and villages all over the country. Those who enlisted were promised that they would serve with other people from their areas.

In Liverpool, Lord Derby appealed for men to enlist in a Pals Battalion. Within three days, over 2,000 men had volunteered, enough for two battalions. This was to be known as K Battalion, The Kings Liverpool Regiment. Liverpool had already supplied nearly 6,000 men to the regular Army and Territorials.

Enlistment in the Liverpool Pals Battalion carried on until November, and by then they had enough men for four battalions, which equalled a brigade. In March 1915 they were inspected by Lord Kitchener and commanded by Brigadier General Stanley, who had helped to recruit them.

Lord Derby and Mrs Stanley, the wife of the brigadier, helped to raise funds in the city to provide comforts for the Liverpool Pals. These included such items as toiletries, playing cards, cigarettes and gloves, no doubt helping ease their entry into France. Strangely, as the idea of a 'Pals Unit' was to fight together, the battalions were

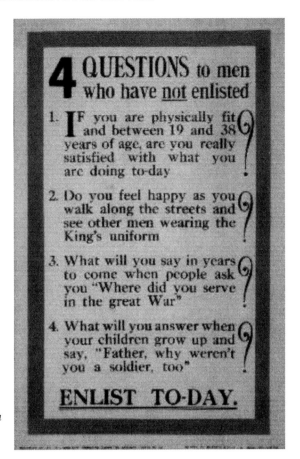

If patriotism was not enough to make men enlist, then guilt was employed.

split up and sent to different areas. The Liverpool Pals took part in many of the great battles of the war, including the Somme. Their losses were so heavy that by 1918 the four battalions had been reduced to three.

The success of the Liverpool Pals was an inspiration to other towns. Serious rivalry grew between those towns that wanted to raise the most recruits. The Accrington Pals began to be recruited in September 1914 and reached battalion levels within ten days. There were several examples of families and workmates enlisting together. A company was even raised for the battalion from the Burnley Lads Club, which had been opened by mill owner, H. Riley, for local working-class lads. Sheffield men were even keener. When recruitment began in September they reached battalion strength in two days. Many of the

Pal's Battalions were from a cross section of society, including men from a wide variety of occupations within their ranks. Officers in the privately raised Pals Battalions were appointed from amongst the more prominent members of the new units. Most had little or no military experience and were often very young. There was an obvious reason for the officers being chosen from the most prominent families in these areas: being an officer was an expensive business. It was estimated at the beginning of the twentieth century that an infantry officer needed more than £150 a year, on top of his Army pay, just to survive. Being an officer in the cavalry was even more costly. It was only a few years before the war that the Government began to supply horses; before this, cavalry officers had to buy their own mounts. The price of an officer's kit was also prohibitive. The well-known tailors, Moss Brothers, advertised in several publications the price of officers' uniforms. A Sam Browne belt was 30s and a coat as much as 63s – beyond the means of most working-class men.

Some battalions were raised from men in similar occupations, or even from the same employer. The Hull Commercials were all from similar occupations. The Glasgow Tramway's Battalion all worked for the same employer. Over 1,000 of the tramway's recruits paraded before the Glasgow City Chambers and were addressed by the Lord Provost. Other units had a common background, such as the Tyneside Irish.

Recruits for the London Regiment, the old 7th Fusiliers, were drawn from men from the London Stock Exchange, banks and city companies. They paraded before Lord Roberts in Temple Gardens at the end of August 1914 and numbered 1,100, but had yet to receive any uniforms.

Pals trained in the new Army camps appeared all over England. A number of these new battalions arrived in France just in time for the Battle of the Somme, and problems quickly became obvious. During the battle, many units were decimated. Out of the 720 members of the Accrington Pals, 584 died. The Leeds Pals had 900 strong men, and 750 died. Other units lost up to half their strength. After the Battle of the Somme, many towns and villages across the country were devastated. Some towns had suffered deaths from families on every street. In Accrington, the whole town was swamped in collective grief.

There were also plans to raise a University and Public Schools Battalion. This came about when a number of ex-public schoolboys found that they were too old for commissions with the first 100,000 recruits, when the age limit was set at thirty years. Their only alternative was to enlist in the ranks but not all ranks were suitable for them. There were always claims that the formation of the UPS Battalion was not due to snobbery. However, many recruits claimed that if they had to spend long hours in the company of other men, they would rather be with men from the same background. There were even plans to have companies within the battalion based on single schools, such as an Eton Company. Of course, many of the men who joined this unit would have been expected to become officers. Because of this, initially there were no recognised officers in the battalion, as they were all of the officer class. It was suggested that they could join the battalion and train while they were waiting for a commission.

The UPS was stationed on Epsom Race Course where they initially enlisted 600 men. The War Office would not take control of the battalion until it reached a strength of around 1,200. It soon reached and surpassed that number and eventually enlisted enough men for four battalions, becoming a brigade. However, they lost over 3,000 men to commissions and, as with other battalions, were 'weakened' by replacements that came from any walk of life.

Age and arrogance were not the only reasons why so many well-educated young men joined the ranks. There were many that were so eager to do their bit that they rushed to the front as private soldiers by the quickest way possible. While the Army was crying out for suitable officer material, vast numbers of obvious candidates were being slaughtered in suicidal infantry attacks in France.

Gentlemen jockeys enlisted in the Hussars, and an idea for an Athletes Volunteer Force also cropped up – perhaps an early version of the Sportsmen. Some Sportsmen were involved in a dispute over whether they should serve or not. Mr F. Charrington, an East End of London temperance worker, started a crusade to get professional football banned during the war. He felt that continuing the games would deter members of the teams from enlisting in the Army. There was a lot of support for his view, but the football league decided to carry on playing.

Another group of men also joined battalions consisting of those with similar occupations or interests. These included such famous units as the Artist Rifles, who counted amongst their numbers several of the better-known war poets. There were also the Post Office Rifles, the

Civil Service Rifles and many others. These units had their origins in the middle of the nineteenth century, when rifle volunteer battalions were formed in response to another threat from political unrest in France. These volunteer units had a middle-class membership before the war, mainly due to the fact that recruits had to supply their own equipment.

Douglas Reed joined the Artist Rifles in the years before the war. He had just become a bank clerk and was moving up the social ladder when he became a Saturday afternoon soldier by joining the Artists. He described the unit as a military formation peculiar to England, as it was reserved for persons of superior social standing. The unwritten law was that only public schoolboys were allowed to join. Reed was somewhat surprised that he was allowed to enrol, as he had not been to public school. He described the situation as 'the cult of the public school at its height', supporting the opinion of the upper classes which asserted that 'the British soldier will follow a public school man into hell but not a ranker wallah'.

In the past, war had seemed to be looked upon as no more than a sport. There was little understanding amongst the public of how this war would differ from those in the past. Famous men such as Sir Arthur Conan Doyle told local men at a meeting that a 'cricketer with a straight eye could look along the barrel of a rifle, and a footballer could use his strength of limb to march into the field of battle.' The Middlesex Regiment already had its own football battalion.

Admiral Lord Charles Beresford called on young men who were still playing sports. He said that he was casting no stones, but men who played football, cricket and other games wre the finest specimens of British manhood. 'They are fit, strong and healthy, and as sportsmen are cheery. Health, vigour and cheerfulness makes pluck.' He impressed upon them the need to be prepared to stand by their country.

Those connected with sports encouraged members of teams to join the Army. The Welsh Rugby Union Committee said that it was the duty of all team members to join immediately. Some teams immediately cancelled all their games so that their members could enlist.

Not everyone looked upon the war as sport. A new weekly newspaper, the *Fatherland*, was published by the Germans but printed in New York. It was then sent by post to some English homes and asked the question, 'Do you want to hear the other side of the argument?' One of the articles in the *Fatherland* was taken from the *Cologne Gazette* and the

Hyde Park was extensively used to drill recruits, as this stereo view of the Citizens Army marching past Lord French shows.

writer was shocked at the use of sporting expressions by the British, described as people on the other side of the North Sea, during the crisis of a world war. The newspaper criticised Sir John French for talking about the absence of fair play. Winston Churchill was also criticised for describing the British Navy as the 'dog' while the German Navy was the 'rat'.

The *Fatherland* stated that Germany would always strive against attempts to measure world affairs as competition between sportsmen and non-sportsmen. They argued that the German mind had given Europe other cultural values, rather than records in tennis and rowing. The British were accused of ignorance in the face of the seriousness of war. For the British, war was an intense, dramatic and profitable sport. Perhaps the Germans had a point: 'War is a game which were their subjects wise Kings would not play at' (Cowper).

Many of the new battalions became part of the Royal Fusiliers. By the end of the war there were forty-four fusilier battalions, and two more were added after the war, totalling nearly 200,000 men. If the London regiments were included, who also had Royal Fusiliers in their title, the number was closer to a quarter of a million. This means that the total number of Royal Fusiliers was greater than the size of the original British Expeditionary Force. It is no surprise that the Sportsmen's Battalion became part of this fusilier group.

There was further great expansion in existing regiments of the regular Army. Many of those who volunteered ended up in regiments that they had not expected to be in. Often, men who volunteered together ended up separated in different units.

When the numbers of men enlisting in the Army increased there was found to be a serious shortage of non-commissioned officers to train them. Lord Kitchener appealed for NCOs with previous military experience. He promised that they would be reinstated in the rank at which they had previously served.

There was a shortage of experienced officers; many were older men who were brought out of retirement. There was a story of a sixty-five-year-old officer who died of a heart attack while on parade. It was said that one elderly cavalry officer had put on so much weight that a horse could not be found which could carry him. Henry Webber of the South Lancashire Regiment was the oldest officer, at sixty-eight years, to die on the Western Front. Lieutenant Webber had three sons who also served as officers. One qualification for new officers early in the war was that they had attended public school or university. It was even better if the applicants were from the same school as the commanding officer. When some men applied for a commission, they were refused, despite being from very good schools, as it had to be a school that was on the recognised list.

It was quite common for recruits to criticise their officers, many of whom seemed to have little idea of what they were supposed to do. There did seem to be a closer relationship between the men and the younger officers who actually commanded the smaller sections, such as companies and platoons, while the rank and file still had less regard for the more senior and distant officers. Much of this trust seemed to be based on the men's regard for their officers being gentlemen. However, the background of many of the young officers was not that of the landed gentry. Many were the sons of lawyers, doctors and even teachers. What they had in common with the more aristocratic officers was public school education.

It may seem strange now, in what is perhaps a more enlightened age, that so many men were persuaded to enlist in a war that was to be so long and dangerous. There seem to have been a number of reasons for this. There were numerous stories in newspapers about German atrocities in Belgium against civilians. Although some now argue that most of these stories were propaganda, there was some truth to them. Civilians were executed in Belgium, usually in retaliation for attacks

Early recruits show a light-hearted approach to conflict, as they toss a new recruit in a blanket.

on German soldiers. The propaganda machine was also at work in Germany where it was reported that crowds of Belgians were capturing and torturing German soldiers.

Until the war came along, literature of the pre-war period depicted an ideal age. Of course this was a largely upper-class view, as life was generally more pleasant for the better-off. What made these people leave this utopian life was a sense of duty.

Life for the working class in pre-war days was not so enjoyable. In the working-class areas many men went to fight because it was a chance of adventure, away from the monotony of hard physical jobs. Although the living conditions in Army camps were not perfect, in many cases they were as good, if not better, than the home-living conditions of the poorest members of society. Even the terrible conditions in the trenches were often no worse than conditions that many men worked in at home. It was not only manual workers who wanted to escape their lives at home. Clerical work at that time was repetitive and stifling, so those of a slightly higher social standing may have had similar motivation for joining up as the working class.

A much greater level of patriotism permeated British society at the time than it does today, a fervour fuelled by stories of German atrocities. Patriotism reached across class barriers. Even those of the masses who had leanings toward class rebellion did not think twice about joining up. Many men had seen their fathers fight in earlier wars, and they believed that it was expected of them. However, during the early days of the war men also lacked information concerning the conditions in the trenches.

Of course, not everyone joined for patriotic reasons. Some men may have joined to impress their girlfriends or wives or to appease their communities, or because all their friends did. And there was always the danger that Germany could invade Britain if not enough men went to fight. What stands out, however, is that most recruits viewed the war as some sort of adventure.

CHAPTER 2

FORMATION OF THE SPORTSMEN'S BATTALION

It was against the backdrop of a country inspired with patriotism that the Sportsmen's Battalion came about. The Sportsmen's Battalion was raised by Mrs Cunliffe Owen, whose family had connections with the highest members of society. She and her husband were related to the Royal family. It should have been quite easy for Mrs Owen to obtain a concession from the king to allow older men of up to forty-five years of age to join. Until then, men of this age had been barred from serving in the war.

Although it looks to have been Mrs Owen who was mainly responsible for the creation of the battalion, her husband's position must have helped. Edward Cunliffe Owen was educated at Wellington College and Trinity College, Cambridge. He was a barrister and had been secretary of the Fisheries, Health and Inventions Exhibition at South Kensington. He was also the assistant secretary for the Indian and Colonial Exhibition for which he received the CMG. Edward was the secretary of the Metropolitan Electric Light Company for thirty years and the only son of Colonel Henry Cunliffe Owen, of the Royal Engineers. His wife was the daughter of Sir Philip Cunliffe Owen – the couple were actually cousins, as well as man and wife. They had two daughters and a son, the godson of Queen Alexandra, who became an officer in the 2nd Sportsmen's Battalion.

Not everyone agreed that older men would make suitable soldiers. When the 10th Essex arrived in France, a shell case landed close to the men as they marched towards the front. One man ran to the shell and picked it up, burning his hand. He reported sick and was never seen

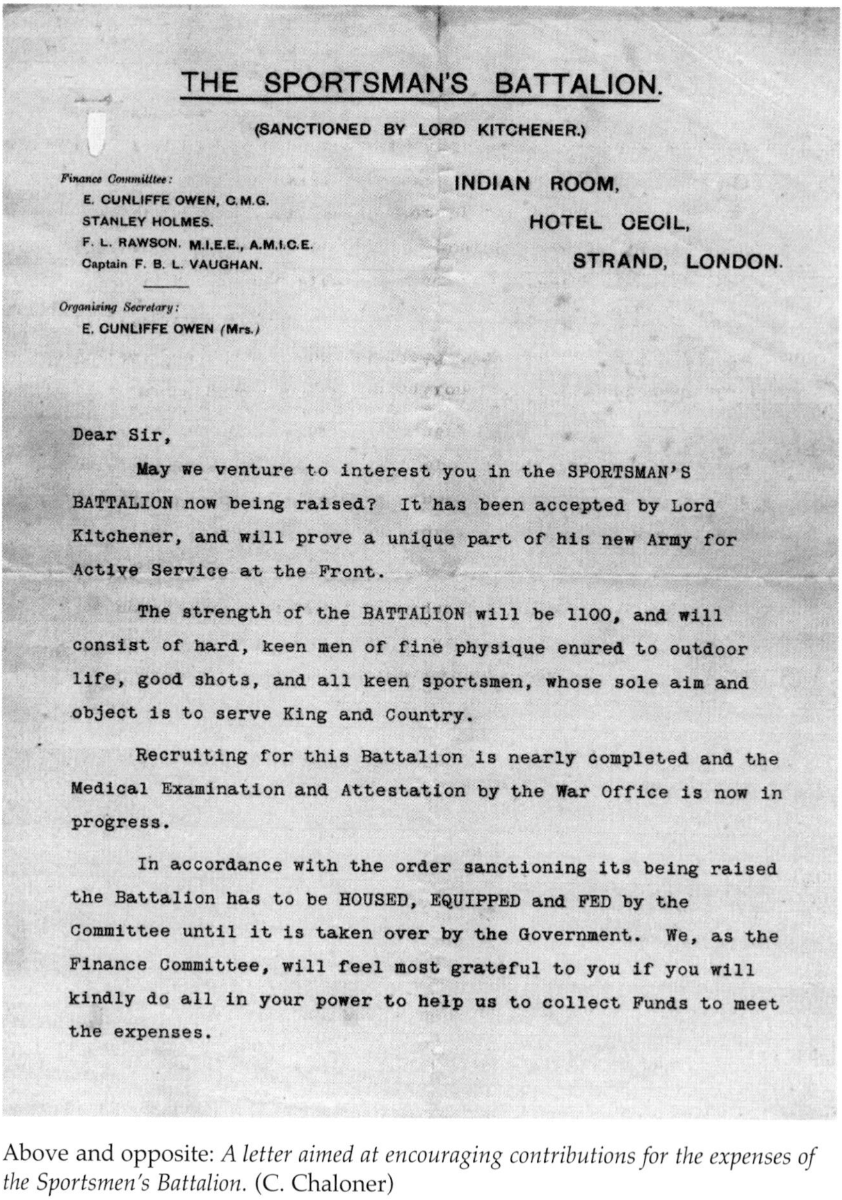

THE SPORTSMAN'S BATTALION.

(SANCTIONED BY LORD KITCHENER.)

Finance Committee :
E. CUNLIFFE OWEN, C.M.G.
STANLEY HOLMES.
F. L. RAWSON. M.I.E.E., A.M.I.C.E.
Captain F. B. L. VAUGHAN.

Organising Secretary :
E. CUNLIFFE OWEN *(Mrs.)*

INDIAN ROOM,

HOTEL CECIL,

STRAND, LONDON.

Dear Sir,

May we venture to interest you in the SPORTSMAN'S BATTALION now being raised? It has been accepted by Lord Kitchener, and will prove a unique part of his new Army for Active Service at the Front.

The strength of the BATTALION will be 1100, and will consist of hard, keen men of fine physique enured to outdoor life, good shots, and all keen sportsmen, whose sole aim and object is to serve King and Country.

Recruiting for this Battalion is nearly completed and the Medical Examination and Attestation by the War Office is now in progress.

In accordance with the order sanctioning its being raised the Battalion has to be HOUSED, EQUIPPED and FED by the Committee until it is taken over by the Government. We, as the Finance Committee, will feel most grateful to you if you will kindly do all in your power to help us to collect Funds to meet the expenses.

Above and opposite: *A letter aimed at encouraging contributions for the expenses of the Sportsmen's Battalion.* (C. Chaloner)

Sir William Plender, of Deloitte, Plender, Griffiths & Co. Chartered Accountants, has consented to act as Honorary Treasurer. Every care will be taken to ensure the proper disposal of Funds entrusted to us, and a full Financial Statement will in due course be forwarded to each subscriber.

Full details of the expenses which have to be incurred are appended, together with the sums to be refunded by the War Office under the Schedule of Regulations applying to this Battalion.

As the Battalion goes into training quarters during the week commencing the 12th inst., and there still remains a great deal to be done before that time, we shall be very grateful if you will do all in your power to assist us as speedily and liberally as possible.

Thanking you in anticipation for your kind and generous help.

We are,

Yours faithfully,

On behalf of the Committee,

E. Cunliffe-Owen.

Organizing Secretary.

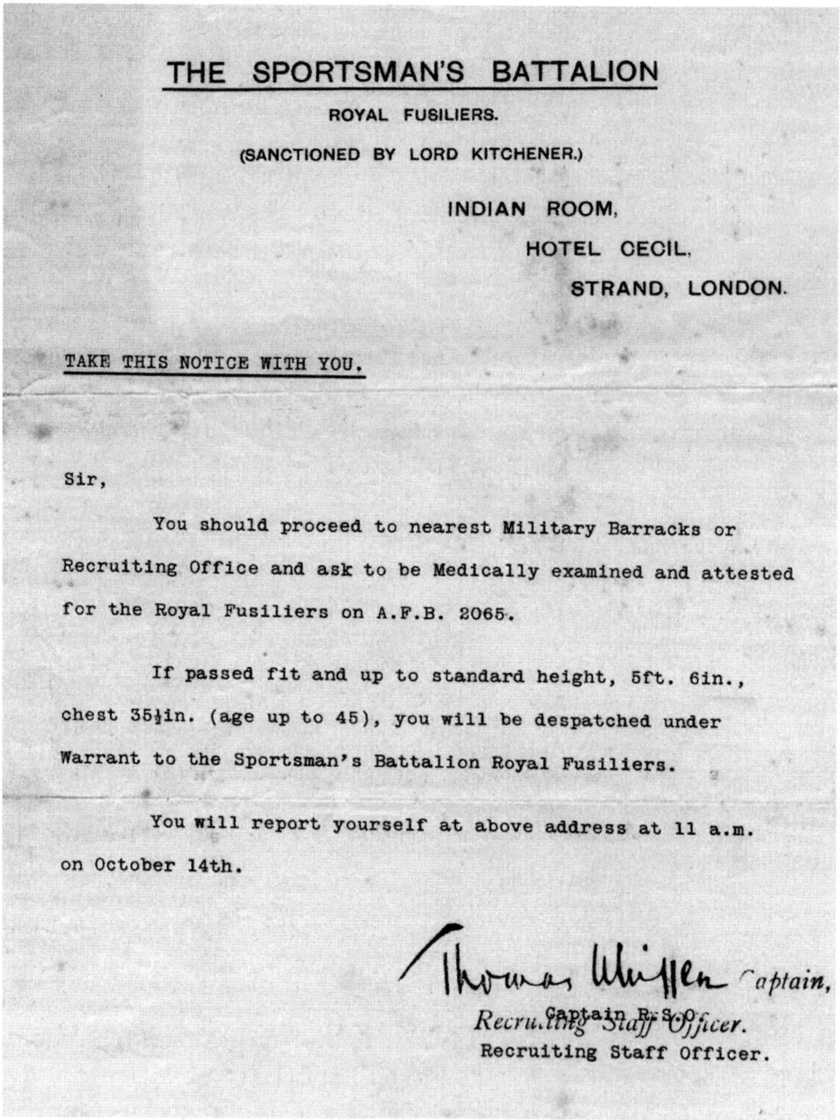

THE SPORTSMAN'S BATTALION

ROYAL FUSILIERS.

(SANCTIONED BY LORD KITCHENER.)

INDIAN ROOM,

HOTEL CECIL,

STRAND, LONDON.

<u>TAKE THIS NOTICE WITH YOU.</u>

Sir,

You should proceed to nearest Military Barracks or Recruiting Office and ask to be Medically examined and attested for the Royal Fusiliers on A.F.B. 2065.

If passed fit and up to standard height, 5ft. 6in., chest 35½in. (age up to 45), you will be despatched under Warrant to the Sportsman's Battalion Royal Fusiliers.

You will report yourself at above address at 11 a.m. on October 14th.

Thomas Whiffen Captain,

Recruiting Staff Officer.

Recruiting Staff Officer.

Instructions to recruits as to how to proceed during a medical. (C. Chaloner) again. The feeling amongst his comrades was that they suffered no significant loss, as he was about forty years old and far too old for war – a criticism that could have been applied to a number of the recruits with the Sportsmen.

To qualify for the Sportsmen volunteers one had to have some level of ability in sport or entertainment. It was the supposed levels of fitness of these sporting men that gave them the 'Hard as Nails' nickname. In those times most sport was still played on an amateur basis, so recruits either had another occupation or were gentlemen of leisure. It did not seem to occur to anyone, when the idea for the battalion was formed, that even if the recruits had been Sportsmen in the past, by the age of forty-five their sporting days would be behind them. As for being involved in the world of entertainment, did being on the stage or being a writer make someone fit?

It may be hard to believe now that a man's sporting history could have been so significant. William Carr had just gained a degree from Aberdeen University when, in January 1916, he travelled to London to go before a board of officers at Lincoln Inn Fields after applying for a commission. One of the questions the board asked was what games did he play at school? Carr said that the officers stared at him in disbelief when he said that they did not play games at his school. He was quickly sent out of the room. He knew from that point he would not get his commission. The letter declining his request arrived a week later.

Emphasis on sport was a deciding factor for men who got a commission and was strongly connected with the ethos of the public school. It is hard to define what this ethos involved exactly, but sporting prowess was a large part of it. Those who went to the best schools were seen to have learnt loyalty, honour, chivalry, patriotism and sportsmanship. Many of the ex-public schoolboys who ran the Army saw these as the ideal qualities for a future officer, even if the applicants were not too bright.

One man reported how he went to apply for a commission and found that the officer who interviewed him had seen him play for Eton at Lords, in the Eton *v.* Harrow schools cricket match. There was no doubt that he must have been suitable officer material and indeed he was accepted. The man's brother had accompanied the applicant and was himself accepted for a commission on the strength of his sibling's prowess at cricket.

The British Army's sporting reputation was well known beyond the shores of England. A writer in the French newspaper *L'Indepenence* said in 1914 that 'the Tommy loves to laugh, smokes continuously and is a sportsman. He views war as a continuation of the sport that he plays during peacetime'.

The sporting image of the public schoolboy had a long history. During the nineteenth century, teachers for the best schools were often recruited from those with a rugby blue, rather than applicants with a good degree. There was a definite bias towards an education that did not necessarily prepare the boys for any useful occupation, as trade was still looked down upon. A strong emphasis on the classics was often queried by ex-pupils but was regarded as an important part of a gentleman's education.

At school, prefects and school captains were chosen from the sporting heroes, not from the more academically minded pupils. The image of an athletic ideal was fed down to the rest of the population through novels about public schools and, in the years before the war, through the cheap comics that began to appear. Most of these were published by media owners who were trying to instil a level of patriotism amongst the lower classes.

Although the working-class boy who read these comics could not hope to be part of the elite who went to public school, he could aspire to behave in a similar fashion. Many of the heroic characters in the comic stories were public schoolboys, but they often had a sidekick who was from the lower classes. He would be portrayed as a steady reliable chap who looked up to his master and tried to emulate his behaviour. This was considered exemplary conduct for men who would be following their masters, the officers, without question through the terrors of the trenches. However, the sportsmen of England were about to find themselves on the largest and muddiest pitch in the world once they got to the front. Once there, they found that rain did not stop play and the enemy did not always play the game according to the same rules.

Naturally not all men took this sporting ideal so seriously. A letter, supposedly from the front, was printed in the magazine *Newnes Illustrated*. The soldier who wrote it said that at the conclusion of a battle which was fought near a river, a fishing competition had been organised for the men. This competition included entrance fees and a cash prize for the winners. The writer of the letter went on to report that due to his usual bad luck he failed to win a prize, owing to the fact that his worm wasn't trying.

SPORTSMAN'S BATTALION

RENT, &C. OF TRAINING QUARTERS	£ 600
HUTMENTS, ACCORDING TO WAR OFFICE PATTERN	£10,000
UNIFORMS, 1,100 AT £8	£ 8,800
RIFLES	
TRANSPORT EQUIPMENT	£ 3,000
RED CROSS EQUIPMENT	£ 1,000
FURNITURE AND GENERAL UTENSILS	£ 1,200
ADDITIONAL BLANKETS	£ 1,050
FOOD 30 DAYS	£ 4,125
LIGHTING, HEATING, TELEPHONES, ETC. ...	£ 3,000
	£32,775

Against this expenditure the amount repayable

by the War Office may be estimated at ... £20,000

Leaving a balance to be found of £12,775

A list of expenses involved in raising a battalion of men to fight in the war.
(C. Chaloner)

There is no doubt that in the early days of the war there was a perception of something almost light-hearted and fun in taking part in the conflict. The barbed wire protecting one German trench was hung with tin cans to sound a warning if anyone approached. A British soldier crept across to the wire one night and tied string to the wire, which he then led back to the English trench. The string would be pulled at regular intervals, setting off the noise of the cans and causing outbreak of heavy gunfire from the German Trench.

The Sportsmen's Battalion was a very popular concept amid this sporting background. There were over 1,500 written applications to join the battalion in September 1914. The recruiting office at the Hotel Cecil was always full of men wishing to enlist. Some of the men who did enlist thought that the Sportsmen's Battalion was to be a cavalry unit and were prepared to supply their own horses.

The Hotel Cecil had already been the site of some significant wartime events. On 2 September, a sympathetic meeting was held in the hotel by the Eighty Club and attended by several members of parliament. The object was to give a send-off to the members of the Belgian Mission who had visited London on their way to America.

The mission consisted of Minister of Justice M. Carton de Wiart, Ministers of State M. De Saedeleer, M. Hymans and M. Vandervelde, and Count de Lichtervelde. They were empowered by the king of Belgium to provide proof of German-committed atrocities during the occupation of their country to the governments of Britain and America.

A letter was sent from the Hotel Cecil by Mrs Cunliffe Owen in September 1914 regarding the formation of a private battalion of 1,300 men who would comprise strong, hearty sporting gentlemen of up to forty-five years of age. There was also a request to the recipient of the letter to inform any of their friends who would also be willing to serve 'King and Country'. Anyone interested was to send details of name, age, height, weight and their medical certificate to the Hotel Cecil.

The original physical requirements for the battalion were a height of at least 5ft 6in and a chest measurement of at least 35½in and the age limit went up to forty-five years. Recruits, the letter went on, also should be of fine physique, accustomed to outdoor life, good shots and keen sportsmen.

Although the requirements for entry may have been quite stringent at first, there was an evident relaxation of the rules, as the number of high-class applicants ran out. As the war pressed on and as casualties began

The Hotel Cecil, one of the better-class recruiting centres and the largest hotel in Europe at one time.

to mount, the men sent to replace them increasingly came from any walk of life. By 1916 there was very little effort made to match new recruits to special units. They would be sent anywhere they were needed.

During October, many of those sportsmen who hoped to enlist in London attended Scotland Yard for their medicals. Only 5–7 per cent failed their physicals, mainly due to poor eyesight. Many other recruits were to be medically examined at the War Office, while those from other parts of the country received their physicals locally before coming to London.

Although the battalion did include several sportsmen, later attempts to recruit more men led to the dropping of the sportsman qualification and listed the entry requirement as simply men from public schools. The idea was that such applicants would thus automatically qualify as sportsmen, if they were public schoolboys.

The battalion mainly consisted of men from wealthy and noble families but who were serving together as private soldiers. However, there were others who were not from such high spheres of society. There were even cases of men from the aristocracy, such as the brother of a peer and his chauffer, both serving together: the model aristocrat with his lower-class assistant, as traditionally portrayed in the comics. There does not,

An inspection of the battalion in Hyde Park by Viscount Maitland, minus uniforms.

however, appear to have been any consistent separation of men within the ranks, whatever their background.

In 1915, the poet Edward Thomas was considering joining the Army. In a letter to his parents, dated 9 July 1915, he said that he was thinking of joining the Artist Rifles, which had by then become an officer training corps. On account of his age, thirty-seven, he would not have been fit for service in the trenches, but if given a commission he could train soldiers in England. His alternative was the Sportsmen's Battalion, although surprisingly he believed that he might find the battalion a rowdy set – no better company than the ordinary crowd of privates. The Artist Rifles were mostly professional men. Perhaps then the reputation of the Sportsmen's Battalion was not quite what it was supposed to be.

The fact that the make up of the members of the battalion was to come mainly from the elite of society was illustrated by the place where they went to enlist. Most soldiers enlisted in local drill halls. The sportsmen enlisted at the Hotel Cecil in London. Despite this regal recruiting centre, the men still had to report to the nearest military barracks or recruiting office for their medicals.

The Hotel Cecil was built in the late nineteenth century. Its construction led to the demolition of two streets, Cecil Street and Salisbury

The Sportsmen were regular visitors to Hyde Park, along with many other London-based units. (C. Chaloner)

Street. The hotel, the largest in Europe, had 600 bedrooms. The main entrance was in the Strand but the front of the building faced the Thames embankment, with gardens running down toward the river. An advertisement in the *Daily Mail* on 5 November 1914 stated that the administration offices of the Sportsmen's Battalion would be at the hotel until further notice.

The exclusive quality projected by the Cecil was shown in one of the radio broadcasts by John Betjeman at a later date. Betjeman was harking back to a time in London's past when the city was more attractive. A joke that he told involved a lady who asked a bus driver if he stopped at the Cecil. He replied, 'Do I stop at the Cecil, what on twenty-eight bob a week?' The Cecil was demolished in 1930 to make way for Shell Mex House, no doubt one of the many tragic exits of icons of London's past.

Mrs Cunliffe Owen took an active part in the recruitment process, aided by a staff that worked very long hours. Lieutenant Winter sat at a green baize covered table with a large ledger recording the names of the men who wished to join. The battalion tailor was also present and had some difficulty with the men's sizes, as they were often well above the average height. The first members of the battalion must have looked like the early Home Guard of the Second World War, as many men wore only part of their uniform as they paraded the streets of London.

Although the battalion drilled in London, many of its members came from areas outside the capital. The majority of these travelled in every morning, mainly by train, and all paying their own fare. There were plenty of volunteers to become a member of the party who were to prepare the battalion's new camp at Grey Towers in Hornchurch, Essex.

The recruits seemed to be eager to get on with the work but with little idea of what the labour would be like and few thoughts in general as to what the future might hold.

Recruitment for the battalion was not limited to London. Captain Whitehead was present from 2 to 7 November 1914 at the Edinburgh Royal Hotel. The previous week he had been at the Glasgow, at the Central Hotel. After November recruitment for the sportsmen in Scotland had ended.

Raising a battalion was not cheap. Everything had to be paid for before the War Office took over responsibility and the total amount needed was £32,775, with the most expensive item being the huts for the men at Hornchurch. Uniforms were also very expensive, mainly due to the oversized and strapping physiques of so many of the men. The War Office finally paid £20,000 of this amount, while the rest was raised by donations, much of it coming from the men themselves. Donations of three guineas were requested from recruits. The finances were managed by the committee, which included Mrs E. Cunliffe Owen CMG, Stanley Holmes, F.L. Rawson M I EE A M I C E, and Captain F.B.L. Vaughan.

The sportsmen were a unique battalion for a number of reasons. Its colours were distinct from the regiment of which it was part. It was also the only battalion organised by a woman and which allowed older men to join. At one point, the battalion was supposedly presented with a remarkable gift – a base hospital at Almers, Chertsey Surrey. It was given by Frank Geiger of Southwick Street, London, who had himself just joined the battalion. However, I have been unable to find any evidence that the house was ever used as a hospital. It later became common for those people with large houses to take in convalescent officers as houseguests, so perhaps this was how it was used.

The battalion was initially expected to comprise 1,100 men, a strength which was achieved within three weeks. There were then efforts to raise

THE SPORTSMANS BATTALION. HYDE PARK. 4TH NOV. 1914.
F. LUFF.   HORNCHURCH

By the time this photograph was taken, the men had uniforms and were close to leaving for Hornchurch. (C. Chaloner)

a second battalion. The new recruitment posters requested sporting varsity men and old public schoolboys for this new battalion. Pay was at Army rates and there was an optional financial obligation to the battalion. A letter was sent from the battalion at the Cecil, dated 13 November, and now bearing the motto 'Sanctioned by Lord Kitchener'. The letter stated that they were waiting for the order of command from the War Office to proceed with the formation of a 2nd Battalion, of which there were already 500 men waiting to enlist.

The 2nd Battalion was placed under the command of Colonel Paget, who had served for twenty-eight years in the Durham Light Infantry. Recruitment conditions were similar to those for the 1st Battalion and the process took place at the Hotel Cecil. For a time, the ballroom at the hotel was used as a drill hall for the 2nd Battalion. The camp for them was to be at Hare Hall, Romford, a few miles from the 1st Battalion camp at Grey Towers.

It would seem that later the entry requirements for the 2nd Battalion may have relaxed slightly again and recruitment tours were taking place in September 1916. At one of these in Hayle, led by Sergeant J.N. Millet, one of the recruits was a golf caddy, rather than a golfer. Ernest Firstbrook became a bandsman and stretcher-bearer in the 2nd Battalion. Firstbrook later received the Military Medal for his service

Above, left and right: *A silver medallion presented to each member of the battalion by the Cunliffe Owens.*

at Deville Wood. He was killed on 13 November 1916, shot while carrying a stretcher.

The battalion chaplin was Revd Sydney Walker. Doctor Walter Hill was appointed medical officer. The battalion even had an honorary dentist, Mr Arnold Gabriel of Harley Street.

All the men who joined the Sportsmen were presented with a small silver good luck medallion. It had the Royal Fusiliers and Cunliffe Owen crests side by side on one face, with a number, which I believe is the owner's battalion number. On the reverse are the words, 'From Cunliffe Owen, October 1914, God guard you'. The first issue of these medals were later withdrawn due to some problem with the message inscribed on them.

Although the newspapers depicted both the Sportsmen's Battalion and the Cunliffe Owens in a very positive light, everything may not have been as rosy as it first seemed in the Cunliffe Owen household. In July 1915, Mrs Owen was ordered to explain why she had not attended court to give evidence in a case between her husband and a butcher of Victoria Street, London. The butcher claimed that he was owed £14 18s 11d by Mr Owen. In what seems a strange decision, the case was found in Mr Owen's favour because he considered his wife extravagant. If he felt this over a butcher's bill, how did he feel about her helping to finance the Sportsmen's Battalion? Mrs Cunliffe Owen was fined £5.

CHAPTER 3

THE BATTALION AT HORNCHURCH 1914

Grey Towers House, in the town of Hornchurch, Essex, had military connections dating back to well before the First World War. The house was built in 1876 by a Mr Henry Holmes after he bought eighty-seven acres of land from his father-in-law, John Waggener, of the Langtons Estate, nearby. The Grey Towers House was described by local historian Charles Perfect as a 'castellated mansion in the style of the 12th century'. It was similar in style to Harewood Hall, in nearby Corbets Tey, where Holmes had previously lived. However, Harewood Hall was older, having been built in 1782 by Sir James Esdaile. Grey Towers House had a black and white marble staircase and the house was well constructed in an old-fashioned style, so much so as to fool members of the press when reporting on its age, after the Sportsmen's Battalion took up residence.

Henry Holmes had raised a battery of local volunteer artillery in 1882. He then became a colonel of the First Essex Artillery Volunteers and later became the deputy lieutenant for the county of Essex. It seems that the colonel was a popular man; the local writer Charles Perfect composed a poem about him called, 'The Colonel'. The first verse read:

> *Four score and three, his eye not dim,*
> *Martial his bearing, tall and trim,*
> *Straight as an arrow,spick and span,*
> *A fine old English gentleman.*

Grey Towers House. Despite its ancient style of architecture, the building was less than fifty years old.

Holmes later bought the Langtons Estate adjoining Grey Towers after the death of its owners. He kept it until 1899 when he sold it to Varo Williams. Langtons was later presented to the local council and still survives in its original condition as the Havering Registry Office.

However, despite his regal bearing as described by Perfect, within two years of the poem being written the colonel was dead. The funeral was a grand affair attended by a detachment of territorials and numerous local dignitaries lining the route from Grey Towers to St Andrew's Church. Both Colonel Holmes and his wife died in the years just before the war began. Grey Towers then stood empty and was sold by auction in June 1914. The children of the Holmes family had spread across the country and the world, although one of them was to return to Hornchurch.

The first military arrivals at Hornchurch were not based at Grey Towers. The 3rd East Anglian Howitzer Brigade, of the Royal Field Artillery, arrived in the town within a few days of war breaking out. The officers were put up at the White Hart Inn, while the men were billeted in the school building on North Street. The guns were left in a field adjoining Dury Falls.

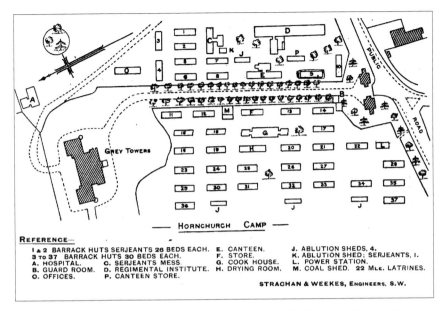

HORNCHURCH CAMP

REFERENCE—

1 & 2 BARRACK HUTS SERJEANTS 26 BEDS EACH.	E. CANTEEN.	J. ABLUTION SHEDS, 4.
3 TO 37 BARRACK HUTS 30 BEDS EACH.	F. STORE.	K. ABLUTION SHED; SERJEANTS, I.
A. HOSPITAL.	C. SERJEANTS MESS.	G. COOK HOUSE.	L. POWER STATION.
B. GUARD ROOM.	D. REGIMENTAL INSTITUTE.	H. DRYING ROOM.	M. COAL SHED. 22 MLE. LATRINES.
O. OFFICES.	P. CANTEEN STORE.		

STRACHAN & WEEKES, ENGINEERS, S.W.

The layout of the camp with huts at Grey Towers, showing both sides of the tree-lined driveway to the house. (C. Chaloner)

Meanwhile, the grounds of Grey Towers were full of hundreds of workmen constructing wooden huts. The buildings were to be completed in a record time of eleven days. What was described as a 'model' Army camp was then opened in October. The local press depicted the huts as almost luxurious, but then they did not have to live in them. The buildings were laid out on named streets. Along with the soldiers' accommodations, there the also other buildings necessary for the running of an Army camp, such as a hospital, guardroom and cookhouse. The civil engineer responsible for designing the camp was Sergeant Weekes, who was also a member of the Sportsmen's Battalion.

John Chessire's first letter to his wife, dated 7 October, was sent from Grey Towers Camp. He described a visit to nearby Romford as being like getting out of prison, after passing the camp gates for the first time since entering them. He mentioned that the men's families were allowed to visit the camp on Sundays. There was obviously no shortage of food in Hornchurch at the time, as in another letter, also posted in October, he stated that he had just returned from town and a hearty supper of sausage and mash.

John mentioned that Government inspectors had visited the camp the previous day and ordered some of the arrangements to be remodelled, which John described as a great relief to everyone. One of these changes was that the men were to have hot coffee before the 7.00 a.m. parade.

In his letter John also brought up one of the officers at the camp, seventeen-year-old Cunliffe Owen. No doubt, becoming an officer at such a young age was due to the influence within the battalion of his parents. The young officer had apparently told the men off because he found soapsuds in one of the fire buckets in a hut. Young Cunliffe Owen was clearly not taken very seriously as an officer. John called him 'a poor boy who tried to remember some swear words but could only utter the word "damn", accompanied by slamming the hut door'. Strangely, Cunliffe Owen does not appear on the original list of officers of the battalion who enlisted at the Hotel Cecil or Hornchurch. I suspected that he must have transferred to another unit but later found him listed as an officer in the 2nd Battalion.

The attitude towards Cunliffe Owen is an example of a difficulty many battalions such as the Sportsmen's must have faced. Other units may have looked up to their officers because they were gentlemen and a class above the normal recruit. However, most of the men of the Sportsmen came from the same class as their officers, so only those who did a decent job in command would earn their respect. As will be further detailed later, many officers ultimately failed in this.

John finished his letter asking his wife to send him pyjamas and tennis shoes. The very fact that John wore pyjamas marked him as in a higher class.

John Chesshire must have been one of the advance party of the battalion sent to Grey Towers, who attended a social gathering at the White Hart Hotel in Hornchurch on 12 October. They were there as the guests of Mr William Batten, the managing director of The American Register and Anglo Colonial World. Those present arranged to repeat the gathering after the war, if they were still alive.

Before the rest of the battalion arrived at Grey Towers, there was a reception held at the camp on 23 October given by Mr and Mrs Cunliffe Owen, with a large company of celebrity guests. The beautiful park land of the estate was turned into a town of wooden huts. Everything was described in the newspapers as 'up-to-date'. There was Royal acknowledgment of the battalion, when Queen Alexandria sent an autographed etching of herself and one of King Edward. These

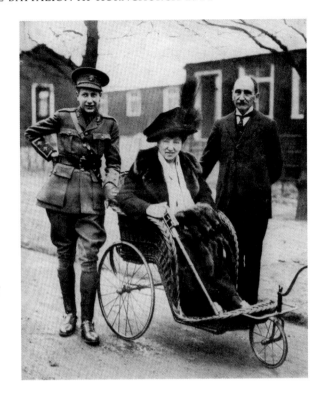

Mr and Mrs Cunliffe Owen and their son Lieutenant Cunliffe Owen at Hornchurch. There is a strong family connection, as Mr Cunliffe Owen was the son of Colonel Cunliffe Owen, and his wife the daughter of Sir Philip Cunliffe Owen.

were hung in the officer's mess, along with the portraits of the then present King George V and Queen Mary.

Huts 1 and 2 had twenty-six beds each and were used as accommodation for the battalion's sergeants. Huts 3 to 37 were for the enlisted men and had thirty beds in each. Other non-residential huts were known by letter, rather than a number. The hospital was hut 'A', and the Guard Room hut 'B'. The huts were laid out either side of the tree-lined driveway leading up to the house. The officers were to be accommodated in the house itself, which seemed to be the norm in such camps.

The day before the battalion was due to leave London, instructions for the men's travel were printed in the *Daily Mail*. They were to assemble in Hyde Park at 11.15 a.m. and to leave by 11.45. For a 'Hard as Nails' Battalion, supposedly accustomed to outdoor living, there was an unexpected footnote to the instructions: 'In case of rain the battalion will leave from the Hotel Cecil.' One would not expect strong men familiar with outdoor life to be worried about rain.

The Sportsmen arriving at Hornchurch on 4 November 1914.

The weather did not affect preparations. Before leaving for Hornchurch, the battalion was inspected by the commanding officer Viscount Maitland. They then marched from Hyde Park, opposite Knightsbridge Barracks, where they had been drilling, to the city through streets lined with crowds of cheering people. The route took them past Buckingham Palace, Wellington Barracks and the Houses of Parliament onto the embankment. They were then addressed at the Mansion House by the Lord Mayor. The *Morning Post* of 5 November 1914 described the scene. The battalion was led by a brass band of the 5th Royal Sussex Territorial Regiment, where large crowds lined the streets and cheered. Many of the men were over 6ft tall and looked so fit that there was no surprise their nickname was the 'Hard as Nails Battalion'. The *Daily Mail* described the parade as, 'a perfect example of the use of pageantry in recruitment'. Handkerchiefs were waved by those watching from windows of the buildings lining the route. Several of the members of the battalion wore medal ribbons from the South African War. Also present was a baronet, a son of a peer and an ex-member of parliament.

The Sportsmen's Battalion travelled by two trains from Liverpool Street to Romford, then marched to their camp on 4 November 1914.

I believe that these are the men from John Chessire's hut at Hornchurch. (C. Chaloner)

Their kit had already gone by road. On one of the vans carrying equipment, someone wrote 'Berlin via Hornchurch'. They were greeted at the gates of Grey Towers House by a large crowd from the town and were led up the tree-lined driveway by the boys of the local Cottage Home Band. The Cottage Home had been built by the guardians of the parish of St Leonards, Shoreditch, in 1889. It provided a village environment for the children in their care and was situated almost directly opposite the camp.

One of the members of the battalion was no stranger to the town of Hornchurch or Grey Towers House. He was Captain Stanley Holmes, the son of the late owner of the estate, Colonel Holmes.

Although the grounds were full of wooden huts for the men, Grey Towers House was used as quarters for the officers. The men were to become a common sight around town after their first fourteen days confined to camp. Part of their training involved morning runs around local lanes. Every Sunday at 9.30 a.m. they would assemble and march to nearby St Andrew's for church parade. The route took them right through the centre of the town. The vicar, the deaf Mr Dale, obviously had a good relationship with the men, as Private Chessire was offered the use of his bath whenever he wanted it.

No doubt, John's religious background had some influence on this friendship. Bathing facilities were evidently one service that was not considered to be especially necessary, even in a modern Army camp. At one church service, the men were treated to an appearance by the Bishop of Chelmsford, who officiated.

The battalion would often march to the station, led by a band and pipers, taking the train to other parts of Essex to undertake trench-digging practice. A short example below illustrates the variety of talents held by members of the battalion:

- Private W. Bates   Yorkshire county cricketer
- Private C. Cambell Rae Brown   author
- Sergeant Major Cumming   champion walker of Britain
- Corporal C.F. Canton   Big Game hunter
- Private Jerry Delaney   lightweight champion boxer
                                                        of England
- Private C.J. Freer   journalist, editor of the
                                                        Sportsman's Gazette
- Corporal Alfred Wharton   comedian

Other regiments would be unlikely to have more than one or two such talented members. Just one hut at Grey Towers had amongst its recruits, a mechanical engineer, a mine overseer who had a pilot's licence, a farmer, a sailor who had sailed round Cape Horn nine times and a bank clerk.

The Hornchurch Cottage Homes band that had led the Battalion into Grey Towers on its arrival was invited to the Picture Pavilion Cinema on South Street, Romford, on 9 November. The manager of the cinema, Frank Coates, invited the band because the film that was being shown was on the Sportsmen's Battalion. There was a further reminder of the war behind the Picture Pavilion, where a rifle range had been opened a few months earlier.

A letter from Private Chessire, dated 12 November, mentions that the camp was inspected by the general of the Eastern District that morning and that no faults were found with his number '9' hut. He wrote that they cancelled the route march that evening because of the rain. Again it seems strange that rain should stop the training of such tough men. The route marches were obviously having an effect, as John reported that 140 men were in the hospital.

John Chessire looked to be a very different person dressed in uniform. The kind persona of the loving family man is no longer evident. (C. Chaloner)

Many of the men were not accustomed to the type of work which was from then on expected of them. One visitor found N. Benjamin, heir to his father's large fortune, scrubbing the floor of his hut. Another recruit, T. Heathorn, well known in the society of the West End of London and an ex-public schoolboy, was the battalion's assistant barber. The youngest recruit, Leonard Skuse, who joined at the age of nineteen, very quickly became a sergeant. Many of the recruits came from overseas to join, from Australia, Canada and the West Indies.

The *Standard Newspaper* reported on the battalion at Hornchurch on 10 November 1914. With literary licence, they described the camp as encircling one of the old stately homes of England, although Grey Towers House was in fact less than forty years old at that time. The battalion was said to consist of 1,270 men who were very keen to get to the front. Sergeant Major Benjamin was described as a giant of a man, who declared that everyone was eager to get into training in order to quickly get to where the fighting was. At every turn in the camp the reporter met men who had won renown in various fields of sport.

Private Clayton Ash, a fellow member of the battalion and friend of John Chessire. (C. Chaloner)

Sport did not come to an end for the recruits when they joined the Army. Private Chessire mentioned that he had joined a rugby team in his letter of 15 November, but did not expect to let it interfere with his military work. He also described a planned route march from Hornchurch to Southend and back.

The men were very much involved in local life while at Hornchurch. Dances and concerts were arranged at the camp, which many local people attended. Many of the concerts were held for local charities. There were also concerts arranged to take place in the town, which the soldiers attended. Other local events that the men took part in were recruiting marches, which took place as far away as Barking and its surrounding area.

Banners appeared outside local businesses reading, 'Welcome the Sportsmen's Battalion'. Locals often turned out in large numbers to watch the men drill, drawn by famous faces within the ranks. There does not seem to have been a great deal of attention paid to security at Army camps during the war. The commanding officer Colonel

*John with his wife
Dorothy and friend
Clayton Ash.*
(C. Chaloner)

(Viscount) Maitland took part in the drills. He was the eldest son of the Earl of Lauderdale and had served in the Royal Scots Fusiliers militia in 1886, and the Dragoons. He was with the Scots Guards in 1894 and had fought in the South African War. Second in command was Colonel Paget. Also present during drills was Sergeant Major McRedmond, an Irishman who came off the retired list to re-join, like many other officers and non-commissioned officers. He had fought in Egypt, India and the Boer War.

The reports in the press painted an idyllic picture of a happy camp, with men totally dedicated to their cause. However, the letters of Private Chessire do not always bear testament to this. In his letter of 25 November, by then written on battalion-headed notepaper, he related that the battalion was again confined to barracks. This was because fifty men had travelled up to London against orders which stated that the men were not to travel more than three miles from camp in case they were needed for coastal defence. There was also an outbreak of diarrhoea, which Private Chessire explained made it very difficult for its victims at night due to a 200-yard walk through the mud and dark to reach the nearest latrine.

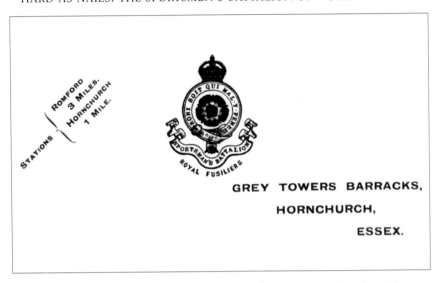

There did not seem to be any attempt at concealing where troops were based, as this letterhead shows, with its listing of the distances from the nearest railway stations.

A few days later Private Chessire recorded his thoughts on the press reports about the battalion and negated their favourable impressions. He described how the camp was seething with complaints due to a combination of bad management, bad pay and bad weather. He wrote that there is 'a lot of nonsense written in the papers' and blamed Mrs Cunliffe Owen for the fact that the supply of non-essential items was good, while the availability of more essential items was poor. However, he did not go into detail as to what these items were.

Many of the activities at the camp had, it seems, been condemned by the War Office. The mistakes learnt at Grey Towers were later put to use in the design of later camps, such as the one at Hare Hall, a few miles away, which became the home of the 2nd Sportsmen's Battalion. There was also a new order given for everyone in the battalion to grow a moustache, which surely had little to do with training to fight the enemy.

A positive camp environment was in evidence at the 1914 Camp Christmas Concert, when the commander Colonel Maitland performed a sword dance, wearing Highland Dress. The close relationship between the soldiers and the locals was proven by the local people leaving their homes on Christmas Day, unusual at that time, to attend the concert at the camp.

The battalion assembled in front of Grey Towers House. (C. Chaloner)

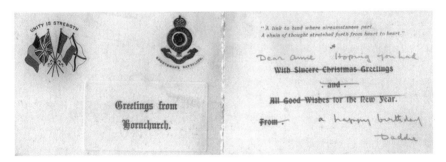

A greetings card from Hornchurch. Christmas cards were adapted for birthdays as well. (C. Chaloner)

A Christmas card from the camp with a patriotic message. (C. Chaloner)

CHAPTER 4

THE BATTALION AT HORNCHURCH 1915

Private Chessire once again revealed the truth about Army life in Grey Towers Camp in a letter sent at the end of 1914. His letter was sent a few days before Christmas but did not arrive until the New Year. The letter was written on headed notepaper with the battalion crest, the address of Grey Towers Camp and the distance from the camp to the nearest railway stations. John explained that there was a gang of thieves operating in the camp and that they had stolen cash and registered letters. Two detectives had arrived in the camp to deal with them. He believed that the gang had been operating since the battalion had been at the Hotel Cecil. Perhaps Edward Thomas had been correct about some of the battalion's members. John mentioned several of the rumours that had been circulating amongst the men.

John commented that it was always raining but that the Canadians had it worse at Salisbury, and that the Sportsmen might be going there to join them after Christmas. He said that the Sportsmen's training was well advanced and that they were much more likely to go to the front before many of the older established regiments. He did not give a reason for this supposition, which, in the event, turned out to be wrong.

The members of the battalion had made great efforts to make the camp comfortable and pleasant. The area around the huts was full of flower pots and gardens that the men had planted themselves. Each hut officially had a number but was also given a name by its inhabitants, which was either spelt out in stones, in the garden outside the hut, or painted artistically on a sign that hung on the wall.

The Camp under Snow.

The first winter at the camp did not bring the sort of weather the men would have wished for.

Guard duty at the gate – note the board with details of the residents and gatehouse with similar design of the house.

The Sportsmen were a good source of publicity, as this page from War Illustrated *shows, with the men pictured reading the magazine.*

Trench digging in Essex came as a surprise to the Sportsmen, but as with all their tasks, they did it well. (C. Chaloner)

A restroom for the soldiers was opened in the school at the back of the Baptist Church on North Street, Hornchurch. This was well used in the evenings by the men from the camp. While at Grey Towers the battalion produced its own weekly magazine, the *Sportsmen's Gazette*. Another connection between the men from the camp and the locals was in sporting competitions. The skill of many of the battalion members must have been intimidating for their opponents.

One activity that came as something of a shock to the men was the digging of trenches. They believed that this was the task of the engineers; as infantry, they assumed they would just stand in the trenches and fight. They were often set to dig trenches near running water so that they learnt to deal with flooding, a vital task, as they were to find out when they later reached France. Luckily, the battalion included a number of civil engineers within its ranks, so they could often correct mistakes.

By the beginning of 1915, the battalion was experienced in the digging of trenches. John Chessire wrote that they paraded each morning at 7.45 and marched to the railway station at Hornchurch. They then travelled by train to Pitsea, near the Essex coast, and marched another three miles before beginning to dig trenches that were to be used for

The digging of trenches was not so urgent as to prevent them stopping for a photograph.
(C. Chaloner)

the protection of London in the event of an invasion. There was a half-hour break for bread and cheese at midday, when, if lucky, they could get a beer at a local inn or a drink of Oxo from a local shop. Then at 3.30 p.m. they began the march back to the station. Later in the month, they moved closer to Southend for more trench digging. Despite the hard manual labour during the day, they still had a good time at camp in the evenings, staying up until 1.00 a.m., even though they still had to rise early the next morning to dig more trenches.

A postcard sent from Leigh-on-Sea the following year mentioned there being plenty of soldiers in the area and noted that there were trenches all along the seafront. No doubt, some of them had been dug by the Sportsmen's Battalion.

While the men were working on trench digging and drilling, the officers were engaged in other important occupations. Major Wolff's diary lists where he was on certain dates, doing a fair bit of travelling around. In January, he was at Aldershot; the following month he was inspecting the 2nd Battalion; and in March he inspected the Essex Regiment at Rayleigh. Whatever advantage officers got from inspecting other units, Major Wolff must have excelled at it.

Page 17   The War Illustrated, 20th February, 1915.

Some Scenes at Hornchurch Training Camp

Instructor-Sergeant Cummings, holder of the world's one mile walk championship (seen in centre), with squad of recruits that he maintains is the finest he has ever trained. Inset on left and right : 2nd Lieut. H. A. Taylor and 2nd Lieut. V. Hayes.

Preliminary hostilities at Hornchurch. Sportsmen pose for their photograph after snowball bombardment of one of the huts.

Lieut. Dr. Walter Hill, chief medical officer to the Sportsmen's Battalion, with "Taxi," the Cruft's winner mascot of the regiment.

Sportsmen seated on a tree that fell, smashing a hut but, fortunately, without injuring any occupants.

The huts at Hornchurch, which accommodate each fifty men. Inset : Lieut. Philip Suckling, first recruit to the battalion, who has served in Zululand.

More scenes of camp life at Hornchurch and the mascot Taxi who, in keeping with groups of winning Sportsmen, was a Crufts-winner himself.

John was expecting a visit from his wife and a weekend pass. He wrote to tell her how difficult it was to get a room in the area for her because so many visitors were coming to see the men. He mentioned trying to get a room at the White Hart Hotel in Romford, where he had dinner the previous evening with Harold Smith, a policeman at Romford Police Station. The inn seemed a popular place for officers and men, as was the inn with the same name in Hornchurch.

The battalion posted in the area provided much new custom for the shops in Essex, and the Sportsmen were not the only units in the locality. This was true of both Hornchurch and the other parts of the county where units were based. One member of the battalion said that local shopkeepers did not put prices up too much for members of the forces because if a local bought shoelaces for a penny, then the Sportsmen were not often charged more than threepence.

In February 1915, Joseph Bysouth, a carriage agent of Milton Road, Romford, was charged in Romford Court with stealing twenty-eight pounds of bacon, three pounds of mutton, seven loaves of bread and a pound of tea from the camp, altogether worth £2. The quartermaster at Grey Towers Camp, Robert De Vere Stackpole, noticed a shortage of rations and instructed the guard at the gate to search all vehicles leaving the camp. When the stolen items were found in two bags in Bysouth's van by the sergeant of the guard, Bysouth claimed that he thought they were rubbish, which he was responsible for throwing out. The canteen at the camp was run by the Peoples Refreshment House Association Ltd, who supplied the food and other necessities for the men. It was their responsibility to clear rubbish, not Bysouth's. Bysouth was remanded on £50 bail.

The beginning of February saw the men being inoculated. John Chessire does not mention which disease this was against, but detailed the effects of the injection as extreme hunger and sleeping sickness. He also wrote about a Zeppelin scare in the area on 2 February. He hoped his wife got back to London before the lights went off, so there must have been some level of blackout because of the Zeppelin.

There were several sports teams within the camp. A Sportsmen's Battalion Association Football Club was formed, with a number of matches between different companies. A league was organised and a cup presented to the winners by Captain Inglis. There were also four rugby teams, one for each company, and a cup presented by Lieutenant

John mentioned outbreaks of unspecified disease at Grey Towers in his letters in February and noted one death. There was another death the following month, when Private Ritchie succumbed. He is buried in Hornchurch Cemetery.

Suckling. Each team featured several men nationally known for their sport. There were also other men who competed in individual sports, such as boxing.

Although many members of the battalion went on to die in France, there were fatalities before they reached the front. Private Edward Willets was a solicitor from Bromley in Kent. He died at the Grey Towers Camp in February 1915 of meningitis at the age of thirty-five. His funeral was held in his hometown and was attended by the battalion band.

Not all the members of the battalion were fit enough for sport. John Chessire described a death occurring in the hospital in his letter of 9 February, which must refer to Private Willets. He believed that it was from the same epidemic that attacked the Canadians suffered from. The newspapers seemed to be more aware of what was happening at the camp than the men there, as the death of Willets was reported in the newspapers before John mentioned it in his letter. He later commented that there had been no more cases of Spotted Fever, but that one man had Scarlet Fever and hut 24 was isolated. By this time the trench digging had moved to Benfleet.

The 2nd Battalion of the Sportsmen was closely connected with the same area of Essex. It was to be billeted at Hare Hall Camp in Romford,

The beginning of the New Year did not stop attempts at recruitment for the battalion, as this poster shows. It is slightly misleading, as the men were still in England, despite what appeared to be happening on the poster.

which was only a few miles from Grey Towers. The arrival of the 2nd Battalion at Romford led to the inevitable football match between the two battalions. The match was played at Romford Town's ground, near the old railway goods yard, but the Romford Town team actually disbanded during the war. The team members from the 1st Battalion were Kirton, Higgins, Follets, Lewis, Littlewort, Baker, Sandham, Bates, Owers, Dobinson and Hendon. The 2nd Battalion team included Taylor, Dunham, Ellis, Guy, McLellan, Kent, Harrowsmith, Lewis, Adams, Rostron and Hoskins.

The crowd was mainly made up of soldiers but there were also a few civilian spectators who watched a closely fought match, which ended in a 2-1 victory for the 1st Battalion.

John Chessire commented adversely on the arrival of the 2nd Battalion. He said that Romford was now too crowded. No doubt it was then even harder to secure a room at an inn for visitors. He mentioned a 'field day', which included a mock battle between the battalions, the results of which he described as disastrous.

The 1st Battalion was involved in other football matches against established teams. In February, the 1st Battalion played Hampstead Town at the Avenue Ground in Cricklewood Lane, and was beaten 3-1. The report in the local newspaper stated that as the result was not entirely acceptable to the Sportsmen, a further match was to be organised. This does not reflect well on the sportsmanship of the upper classes. One would expect such defeat to be accepted with good grace.

This return match took place in March, and again the local paper reported that the Sportsmen were an excellent attraction and the fine combination of athletes provided an enjoyable and keenly fought game. Once again, the result did not flatter the Sportsmen. This time, Hampstead Town won 3-0, and it was the Hampstead's good defence, not a lack of skill, that led to a lack of goals by the Sportsmen. Owers was mentioned as one of the Sportsmen's stars, as was Higgins of Queens Park Rangers. Other team members included Littleworth, Higgins, and the Hendren brothers. The local newspaper described the team as comprising some of the leading footballers under military training, and Hampstead was one of the few teams to beat them. Another game was organised to take place on Easter Monday between Hampstead and the 2nd Sportsmen's Battalion.

John Chessire had to report sick one day at the camp and found that men reporting with him, suffering from colds or flu, were kept waiting

The luxurious homes that the men returned to after a hard day of trench digging.

in the cold for over an hour to see the medical officer. He said that they were ill when reporting but were very sick by the time they did see the doctor.

While at Hornchurch, Chessire was working on a system of signalling, which he described as being very difficult to learn. According to him, the Spion Kop Disaster was due to poor signalling. He had an idea which involved a disc with letters, which would be fitted to a glove on each hand. He then passed the idea on to a Mr Chandler, the manager of Gamages, for development. He was very inventive, as well as being a talented artist, and designed other items, such as a dogcart for carrying a machine-gun and a railway train defence system.

Chessire tellingly remarked that the men were sick of their officers. One member of the battalion said it would be better to blow his brains out than to follow them to the front. The willingness of the British Tommy to follow a public school man into hell seemed to be lacking amongst the Sportsmen.

By the end of April, the training began to involve more than just digging trenches. The battalion was practising how to attack the trenches with bayonets. The method was to advance at the double with the rifle at the trail, and when ten yards from the trench come on guard and jump the trench sticking the sacks as you landed. John never mentioned

71

firing practice when writing about the training. It seems that shortage of ammunition early in the war restricted the opportunity for this.

The men also took the opportunity to practice sleeping outside. This was done in nearby Hainault Forest. By then, another rumour circulated that the battalion was to move to a new camp at Ripon on the following Monday.

The battalion, including its band, formed a guard of honour at the funeral of a local Hornchurch man on 6 May 1915. Private Alfred Hills had been a choirboy at St Andrew's Church in the town. He was wounded on 22 April while serving with the South Winnipeg Rifles and died in a hospital in Oxford on 2 May. He was buried with full military honours in the churchyard at St Andrew's.

Chessire wrote about the level of bomb damage inflicted by a Zeppelin at Southend. He believes that some of the bombs fell on the trenches they had dug at Pitsea. Bombing civilians shocked the public, which was unprepared for a direct threat such as this. John suggested that German prisoners of war should be stationed at the explosive works at Kynocktown near Canvey Island, which was a clear target for the bombers. This was the only occasion when John seemed to have shown rancour against the Germans. Bombing civilians was simply not playing the game.

When the battalion arrived at Grey Towers the previous November, the commanding officer believed that their training could be completed within three months. The fact that this did not happen was not for the want of trying. A typical day had reveille at 6.15 a.m. and parade at 7.00. There was the physical drill until 8.00 a.m. and breakfast until 9.30. Then there would be three hours of military drill before dinner, which lasted from 1.00 p.m. until 2.30. Another two hours of drill took place until 4.30 p.m., when there would be a half an hour for tea before a route march. The evenings were often spent in boxing, wrestling and rifle drill. Three times a week the men were taken to nearby Romford for hot baths or swimming.

Despite the attempts at making the camp comfortable, the training the men received prevented them from having an easy life. The battalion had a name to live up to and so seven-mile marches to the training site were the norm. A day's work and seven miles of marching back was not an uncommon daily event. The time the battalion spent at Grey Towers often seemed to drag on. One well-worn joke that circulated the huts was that after the war, two War Office officials were discussing how it had finished. One asked how the Sportsmen's Battalion had fared during the

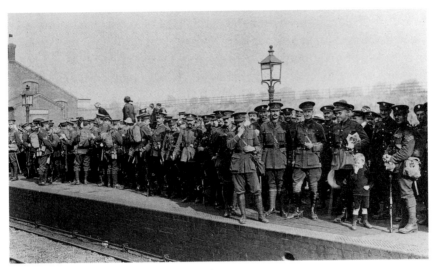

The battalion often marched to the local station at Hornchurch and took a train to other parts of Essex for training.

conflict and the other answered, 'I forgot about them. They are still at Hornchurch'.

At the end of May, the battalion went on a fourteen-mile march to Laindon Hills, which Chessire described as the highest point in Essex and with a wonderful view over the Thames Estuary. They spent the night there before marching back the next day to North Horndon for another night out and then back to Hornchurch the following day. Another rumour was by then circulating about the battalion possibly moving to Aldershot. John got word back about his semaphore glove which, although considered a good idea, would have been detrimental to the sale of the present signalling publications. After all, Polden's had a monopoly on all Army work, which they were not willing to put at risk by allowing new ideas to be developed.

Many of the men who joined the battalion as private soldiers would have, in other regiments, expected to become officers. A problem did arise within the battalion in that some members believed that they would get to the fighting faster if they became officers. This was an interesting and opposing view to that of the ex-public school men, who had initially joined as private soldiers to get the front more quickly.

There was then a rush of applications to the commanding officer to apply for commissions. This exodus could have seriously weakened the battalion, so the colonel introduced a rule that all applicants for commissions had to supply two other recruits to replace them. Because so many men were leaving to become officers in other regiments, this disrupted training and all those waiting for their commission to be confirmed were formed into one company. The company became known as the Essex Beagles, a local sporting club, because instead of parading, they met. The Beagles carried out most of the fatigues at the camp, so that the training of other members of the battalion would not be disrupted.

Although was apparently a great wave of patriotism that led so many men volunteering to fight in the war, this feeling was not universal. In fact, a local man who had previously stood as a candidate for Hornchurch Parish Council, Albert Arthur Ball, was far from patriotic. He was charged under the Defence of the Realm Act for proclaiming that England was behaving in a dirty manner and deserved all it got from Germany. He was sentenced to two weeks' hard labour.

The battalion's last few weeks at Grey Towers was spent on numerous route marches, usually with a night spent camping out. They went to Ongar for a night, which pleased Chessire because of the history of the area. They then marched to to Southend, spending one night on Laindon Hills. The next day they marched back to Hornchurch without another overnight stay.

Towards the end of June, the battalion was given new ammunition wagons, machine-guns and rifles. Once again there were rumours of a move, but this time there was more substance to them. On 21 June, Chessire wrote to his wife saying that an advance guard from Grey Towers had supposedly gone to Ripon and that his luggage had already been taken. There were also rumours that they were in fact going to Nottingham. John guessed that they would join with the 2nd Battalion and the UPS Battalion. When they did leave Hornchurch, there were two companies left behind, D and E Companies.

The esteem that the local people felt for the men of the battalion was vividly shown on the morning they left Hornchurch. Despite it being very early, 6.15 a.m., the streets of the town were lined with the local population gathering to see them off. The following is an excerpt from the *Sportsman's Gazette*:

> Beautiful weather favoured the dawn of the 26 June, the day when the great majority of the Sportsmen's Battalion took their departure from the little Essex village where they had been encamped for the past nine

The end of the Sportsmen's days at Hornchurch arrives as their pipers lead them away.

months. They marched away amid enthusiastic cheers from the whole population.

Not only had the locals turned out, but so did Mrs Cunliffe Owen who had driven down from London to witness the departure. The battalion was led by Colonel Maitland mounted on his horse. The rector of St Andrew's had delivered a farewell address to the men on the camp parade ground. He told them that it was with the regret of the parishioners that the Sportsmen were leaving the town.

A letter from Private Leonard Knight written many years later stated that most of the men believed that they were on their way to France on the morning they left Hornchurch. Instead, they were sent to Clipstone Camp, near Nottingham. The companies that were left behind eventually moved to Hare Hall Camp in Romford to join those of the 2nd Battalion who had stayed behind. The Sportsmen were replaced at

THE SPORTSMAN'S BATTALION LEAVES FOR BERLIN.

Keeping his hut sign as a souvenir.

Waiting for the train.

En route for Berlin.

The Sportsman's Battalion has evacuated Romford, Essex, and fallen back on Nottingham, the operation being carried out in a most orderly fashion yesterday. The next move will be to Berlin.

Once again there were no attempts at secrecy, as newspapers reported where the Sportsmen were off to. The men themselves were not so sure.

the Grey Towers Camp by the Middlesex Regiment, but their stay lasted only a few months. The next residents were soldiers from New Zealand, including several Maoris. Grey Towers became a hospital for the New Zealanders who were recuperating from wounds and illness.

Hornchurch was also the base of a famous airman at nearby Sutton's Lane Aerodrome. In the first few years of the war, the Zeppelins bombed the south-east almost at will, as the firepower of earlier-built planes were not good enough to destroy them – that is, until 3 September 1916 when a pilot from Hornchurch Aerodrome in Sutton's Lane shot down the *L21*. William Leefe Robinson became an overnight celebrity. He received the Victoria Cross from the king, and his face adorned the newspapers and magazines, as well as numerous postcards. Ironically, two other Zeppelins were also destroyed

A stereo view of the battalion marching through the town of Hornchurch for the last time.

shortly afterwards by aeroplane. On 23 September Lieutenant Sowery, another Hornchurch man, brought down the *L32*. On 1 October, the *L31* was shot down by Lieutenant Tempest, also from Hornchurch.

The people of the town made a collection, and on 14 October 1916 silver cups were presented to the three airmen at Grey Towers Camp, which by then had become the base of the New Zealand Army.

CHAPTER 5

THE 2ND BATTALION

On 17 March 1915, the 2nd Battalion was inspected by General Kellet, the commander of the brigade. They were paraded on Horse Guards Parade, Whitehall, before they left for Liverpool Street Station, and then on to Hare Hall in Romford. Kellet carried out the inspection in front of a large crowd of civilians and congratulated the men on their appearance. He said that if they put their backs into it they would quickly become a very efficient battalion, and there would be none better at crushing the Germans.

Earlier in the war, Romford had become a very busy place, with several different Army units based in the town. Many of the men were billeted in local homes and schools. Billeting officers had been in the town in 1914, but even the princely sum of 2s and ninepence per soldier a day was not a great incentive for householders to accept soldiers into their homes. In Gidea Park, east of the town, several new houses had already been built on what had been previously the grounds of a large old stately home. One of these new houses, the Tudor House in Reed Pond Walk, which belonged to the Gidea Park Estate Co., was being used by fifty men of the King's Royal Rifles as a billet. When the men were ready to leave the house, a fire started in one of the bedrooms, gutting the building.

Most of these new houses were built on the site of Gidea Hall. Close by was another old house, Hare Hall. Instead of building houses on the estate belonging to Hare Hall, a large Army camp was constructed. The hall had been the home of Major G. Castellan and Victor Castellan, who were both serving with the Royal Artillery.

The Sportsman's Battalion

ROYAL FUSILIERS

Colonel-in-Chief—THE KING.

is now training at Hornchurch, Essex, and a finer body of men never existed, for every man has fitted himself for the hard life of the soldier by a vigorous life of sport.

The War Office has sanctioned enrolment of recruits for a

2nd Battalion

Sporting Varsity men and Old Public School Boys from 19 to 45 years of age should enlist at once. The 1st Battalion attained full strength in less than 3 weeks.

HOW TO JOIN.—Candidates should in the first instance apply in person or in writing to the Chief Recruiting Officer, Indian Room, Hotel Cecil, London, for Enrolment Form, which, when duly approved at Headquarters, can be presented at the nearest Recruiting Office, when candidates will be immediately examined and attested.

Pay at Army Rates.   *Financial obligation optional.*

Join the Sportsman's Battalion and show the King's enemies what British Sportsmen are.

P.C.R.—12

The 2nd Battalion was looking for men to show the king's enemies what British Sportsmen were made of.

Right and below: *The Hotel Cecil became, not only a recruiting office for the 2nd Battalion, but a drill hall as well.*

The layout of the new camp and huts was very similar to Grey Towers. There was room for about 1,200 men. Hare Hall Camp was, however, described as most commodious and modern, comprising luxuries such as showers, which had not been provided at Grey Towers. These improvements were due to the War Office adaptations to what they had seen as an ideal camp six months previously, at Grey Towers. At the time of the 2nd Battalion's arrival rumours spread of an enlistment of a third battalion. Mrs Cunliffe Owen was still at the Hotel Cecil recruiting; a letter sent from the hotel, dated 6 April, states that only about fifty more men were needed to complete the enlistment of the 2nd Battalion and that they may be asked to form a 3rd Battalion. As had happened with the 1st Battalion, there were many recruits with strong local connections.

Sir Herbert Raphael, the minister of parliament for South Derbyshire, joined the 2nd Battalion as a private. Sir Herbert had previously lived at Gidea Hall, a close neighbour to Hare Hall, whose grounds were at that time being used for building houses. He had twice unsuccessfully stood as the liberal candidate for Romford in general elections. Sir Herbert was also instrumental in developing the Gidea Park Estate, which covered much of what had been the grounds of Gidea Hall, and later went on to do the same to the grounds of Hare Hall. The local park had also been part of the grounds of Gidea Hall and had been given to the local council by Sir Herbert's family. It is still known as Raphael's Park. The park was very popular with soldiers, frequented as a pleasant place for a stroll.

Building on the grounds of Gidea Hall had begun a few years before the war. An article in the *Graphic* in May 1911 described the houses in glowing terms. The Romford Garden Suburb had been laid out around Romford Golf Course and was to eventually accommodate 20,000 inhabitants. There were some connections with those responsible for Hampstead Garden Suburb, and Sir Herbert provided 1,000 guineas in prizes to hold a competition at Romford for architects to design houses costing £350 to £500. The site covered 400 acres and was described as a beautiful area of venerable trees and historic associations. The new residents must have been very surprised to find themselves with numerous military neighbours a few years after the houses were built. The historic associations of the area were not quite finished, as a new chapter was about to begin.

When the 2nd Battalion finally arrived, they had marched from Horse Guards Parade to Liverpool Street Station, and travelled in two

Hare Hall was unlike Grey Towers, which was a fine old house with a history stretching back hundreds of years.

trains to Gidea Park Station. They were welcomed to the area by a large crowd and looked very smart in their uniforms, with white gloves tucked under their shoulder straps. The first detachment was led to camp by the drum, fife and bugle band, and the second detachment was led by a brass band.

Local interest was mainly reserved for Sir Herbert Raphael, who was supposed to be amongst the ranks of private soldiers. Once again, their 'Hard as Nails' nickname seemed to be in question, when it was reported that Sir Herbert could not be present on the march due to his suffering from a heavy cold.

The question of Sir Herbert's service was raised in parliament in February 1915, when it was reported that Lady Raphael was in receipt of a War Separation Allowance of 16s a week. This occasioned a laugh in the house, when it was said that at least Lady Raphael would not be in financial difficulties. The money was in fact given to charity and Sir Herbert explained that he joined as a private because of a lack of military experience, and as an example to the people of Gidea Park. Sir Herbert had a sensible approach to military service, despite the fact that numerous other men were joining the Army as officers, with

A relaxing time at Hare Hall Camp for members of the 2nd Battalion.

not only no military experience, but little experience of anything apart from school which many were not long out of.

Local newspaper the *Romford Times* reported that the 2nd Battalion had acquired two new recruits just before arriving at Romford, two well-known sporting figures. These were Revd George Robinson from Exeter and Revd Sylvester Lee from St Agnes. There were celebrities within the ranks of the 2nd Battalion. One of these was Frank Heath, who was one of the Lamorna artists. Lamorna was a small fishing village in Cornwall which became popular with several artists of the Newlyn School. Frank enlisted with other artists, such as Joey Carter-Wood and Benje Leader. Leader later died in France.

Heath was the youngest of twelve children, and suffered chest problems as a boy. He had exhibited at the Royal Academy as early as 1904. The documents relating to Heath in the Imperial War Museum state that he enlisted in Lady Cunliffe Owen Lister's 2nd Sportsmen's Battalion. While at Hare Hall, he wrote a letter to his daughter which included several small drawings, including one ostensibly of Hare Hall but was actually Balgores House, a nearby building that had been the home of the secretary of the local golf course until given up for the use of officers at the camp. Heath was gassed in France and came home suffering from cerebral meningitis. He was invalided out of the Army and returned home to Cornwall.

The officers of the 2nd Battalion at Hare Hall Camp, including Lieutenant Cunliffe Owen.

Another of the recruits found that whether or not you became an officer often came down to which school you attended. Private W.S. Ferrie was a minister at the United Free Church in Hamilton, Scotland. His father was a Burgess of Coxdale, in Dumbartonshire. Private Ferrie had attended Glasgow University and tried to join the Inns Of Court Officer Training Corps. Unfortunately, the Inns of Court did not recognise Glasgow University as one of their recognised establishments for suitable officer candidates. Ferrie instead joined the 2nd Sportsmen and was with them when they arrived at Romford. His letters in the Imperial War Museum provide some enlightening insights into the Sportsmen. There was a voluntary subscription of three guineas, payable by recruits, which was waived for him. He mentioned that there was a sixty-four-year-old man in the 2nd Battalion but that the man had told them he was forty-five years old. Ferrie had also been told that there were three members of the Anglican clergy in the battalion as well as a millionaire who turned out to be Sir Herbert Raphael. Ferrie had met Sir Herbert at the Hotel Cecil while the battalion had been drilling in London. Of course, Sir Herbert did not join them on the march to Hare Hall.

The time spent at Romford seemed to be very enjoyable for Ferrie. The men would walk to Romford in the evenings and also during the day. Ferrie attended part of the football match between the 1st and

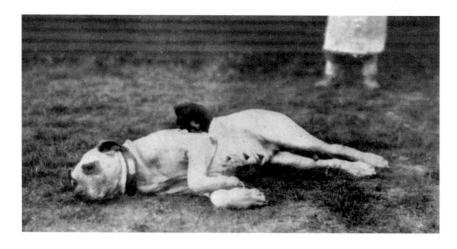

This and opposite page: *Training and relaxing with the 2nd Sportsmen at Hare Hall Camp. There were also two resident dogs at Hare Hall.*

2nd battalions at Romford. It was quite common for men in the Army to visit local factories or places of interest and Ferrie and some other members of the Battalion were shown around the famous brewery in the town.

Ferrie spent some time in the hospital at the camp. His fellow patients included a parson's son, a farmer, a man from India and another from South America. The men all had very different attitudes to the world. They found little time to read or relax, as conversation between them flowed.

Training for the 2nd Battalion at Romford followed similar lines to the 1st Battalion at Hornchurch. The men would march to the railway station in the morning and take a train to Wickford, then march for an hour to their place of work where they would dig trenches. Ferrie believed that this had less to do with training and more to do with getting the job done on the cheap. The trenches were part of the defences for North London. Wickford was only twelve miles from Maldon, which had been damaged by bombs during a Zeppelin raid. Whether this was part of the training or not, it obviously had an effect on Ferrie, as he said he felt as though he could eat a horse and fight a lion. While digging trenches, they would get a half-hour break for a lunch of bread and cheese, usually at a local inn. Sir Herbert often paid for beer and cigarettes for his friends there.

There were never special privileges given to any of the private soldiers in the 2nd Battalion, except perhaps for Sir Herbert, who was seen going out with a lady in his own car – but by then Sir Herbert was no longer a private, but a lance corporal. He was not the only politician in the battalion. Captain Dunn was an ex-minister of parliament and ex-mayor of Exeter.

Ferrie was very active and serious in his religion and often took part in services at the Congregational Church in Romford. His congregation included members of his battalion, other soldiers billeted in the area and the public in general. This led to friendships with local inhabitants of the town, especially with a Mr Harper, who was a brewer. He took Mrs Harper on a tour of Hare Hall Camp.

Ferrie took his religion very seriously and often found the behaviour of his fellow soldiers quite disturbing. He mentioned how the men would go into town in the evenings and attempt to make friends with the local girls. He felt the behaviour of the local girls in Romford was especially cheap, and that the men cheapened themselves by associating with them.

It was not only the 1st Battalion that had to dig trenches. Here the 2nd Battalion take their turn.

While at Romford, Ferrie's father was trying to get him a commission. Ferrie himself was hoping for this but had to speak to the colonel before he could hope to try for a commission. Failure to do this could lead to his being disbarred from becoming an officer. Becoming a non-commissioned officer in the Sportsmen's Battalion was seen as equal to becoming an officer in another regiment. However, he thought the Sportsmen's officers a miserable set.

In May, Ferrie heard some surprising financial news relating to Mrs Cunliffe Owen. She was to appear in bankruptcy court. He hinted that three guineas that recruits were asked to pay (and from which he was exempt) were slightly suspicious. Mrs Owen's patriotism might not have been above dispute. There seems to be some connection in Ferrie's mind between this event and the withdrawal of medals given by Mrs Cunliffe Owen to the 1st Battalion. These were recalled, due to an ambiguous inscription which read something like, 'From Cunliffe Owens and what they're owing'. Different medals were later distributed to the members of the battalion.

Ferrie described Hare Hall as holding 1,400 men, with forty to a hut. When the battalion left to move to Clipstone Camp with the 1st Battalion, about 200 men were left behind, including Ferrie. Both

The Congregational Church at Romford where Private Ferrie took the services for local people and members of the battalion.

The non-commissioned officers of the 2nd Sportsmen's Battalion at Hare Hall Camp.

battalions were well over strength. There was talk of the men left at Hornchurch joining those at Romford to become the 3rd Battalion.

In July, Private James Lambert Jenkins of the 2nd Battalion died at Hare Hall Camp. He had been thought to be suffering from a leg sprain, but suffered a number of fits which caused his death. Evidence was given at the inquest by a local doctor, William Stuttaford, of the Lodge Romford, who was the medical officer of the camp. Jenkins was twenty-five years old and came from Cornwall. He was given a full military funeral and buried in Romford Cemetery. The battalion chaplin Revd H. Curtiss presided over the funeral and three volleys of rifle fire were shot over the grave. Ferrie was one of the funeral party that took part in the military display. He was moved by the actions of the local people, who removed their hats as the funeral passed, but found the slow march, the reverse of arms, the playing of the last post and the three volleys over the grave to feel very false. He afterwards considered that perhaps this reaction was a result of his having to concentrate so hard on playing his part in the ceremony.

Ferrie stayed at Romford until August when he finally received his commission and transferred to the Argyle and Sutherland Highlanders and moved to Ripon. There was another connection between a man from the camp and one of the locals in August. Captain Harold Trim, from Wimbledon, married Mary Elizabeth Laura Teddon, of Laureate, Como Street Romford, at St Edward's Church in Romford Market

Place. Captain Trim was stationed at Hare Hall Camp and the service was carried out by Revd H.B. Curtess.

Not all of the Sportsmen had positive effects on the local population of Romford. A Miss Amy Paterson, a teacher of Eastern Road, Romford, had befriended a man from Hare Hall, but this relationship did not lead to marriage. Private Bernard Towers, of the Royal Fusiliers, was sent for trial at Essex Quarter Sessions for stealing a coat, a gold watch and chain from Miss Paterson. He sold the watch at Porrits, the pawnbrokers on the High Street.

Meanwhile, in Romford, there had been a development with those members of the 1st and 2nd Battalion who had been left behind. At some point they became the 30th Sportsmen's Reserve Battalion Royal Fusiliers instead of the 3rd Sportsmen's Battalion. The new unit kept up the Sportsmen's image and played a cricket match in Romford against the local railway employees in August, which they won.

The month of October was the anniversary of the formation of the 1st Sportsmen's Battalion. This was marked in Romford when the 30th Reserve Battalion held a celebration dinner at H.R. Edwards restaurant, at Gidea Park, attended by thirty-one NCOs and men, including the editor, A.E. Snodgrass, of the *Sportsman's Gazette*. One of the men called for the formation of a Sportsmen's Club in London after the war. The men were led home to camp by the 30th Battalion band.

Later in the same month a concert was held in the Drill Hall, in Romford Market Place. There were several singers and comedians who took part, including Private G.H. Breerton, who sang his recruiting song, 'Aren't You Going to be a Soldier Daddy?'. A large audience attended and helped raise funds for the battalion band.

A November letter, written by a member of the King's Royal Rifle Corps from Gidea Park, a battalion of the Sportsmen and a brigade of the Royal Field Artillery, went to the Dardanelle's from Romford. It said that it was 'fine to see about a mile of guns moving along the road'. The letter also touched on some interesting subjects, such as the news of the deaths of two men during bayonet training in Aldershot. The result was that bare-blade fighting was discontinued during training. The men from the camp went out about three evenings a week and walked into town, or went to Romford YMCA, which had all kinds of games and concerts. The original YMCA in the town had proven to be too small for the increase in the number of soldiers in the town. It was transferred to Wykham Hall, next to St Edward's Church, but even this became too small and was then

Famous Sportsmen Who Have Fallen on the Field of War.

The Sportsmen's Battalion did not have a monopoly on sportsmen who served in the war. These famous men had already fallen while the Sportsmen were still in England.

Field kitchens in Romford and their transports in the background.

transferred to the Corn Exchange. In the camp, the writer also went to the YMCA hut and sewed on buttons or simply chatted. He and three Sportsmen were evidently converted by the Salvation Army. It seems then that there were still some of the Sportsmen at Romford at that time.

The Sportsmen must have left soon afterwards, as a familiar face returned to Hare Hall Camp in December: former Private Ferrie, of the 2nd Sportsmen's Battalion. Ferrie had been commissioned into the Argyle and Sutherland Highlanders but returned to Hare Hall as a member of the Artist Rifles Officer Training Corps, who had now taken over the camp. The camp had not seen its last celebrities, even though the Sportsmen had left. Among the members of the Artist Rifles, based at Hare Hall, were the war poets Wilfred Owen and Edward Thomas.

Ferrie reported that the training at the camp was very good and that lectures were given by the former director of Sandhurst Military School. The camp was a different place than it had been when it was home for the Sportsmen. There were now only twenty-five men to a hut, instead of forty.

A report in the *Waterford News* of 18 February 1916 told how four men had volunteered for the Sportsmen's Battalion. J. Brophy, M. Doyle, C. Dowling and George Jones, captain of Waterford Rugby Club, had all joined the 30th Battalion. The battalion was by then stationed in Oxford.

CHAPTER 6

THE BATTALION AT MANSFIELD

New bases for the rapidly expanding Armed Forces were appearing at points all over the country in the early years of the war. Construction of a massive Army camp began in December 1914, called Clipstone Camp, near Mansfield. The land for the camp had been made available by the Duke of Portland. His decision had not been popular with all the locals.

The impending arrival of thousands of soldiers in any area must have been worrisome for the resident population. A local official in the Clipstone area, Councillor Houfton, spoke out against the construction of the camp at a public meeting in January, and said that if religious and social organisations ignored the soldiers who were soon to arrive, then Mansfield would become a hell. Occupying so many young men in their off-duty hours was a common problem that many towns throughout England faced. In the rural areas that became sites for new bases, there was little in the way of entertainment for the young men who had been sent there; something that could often lead to the men becoming embroiled in mischief and drunkenness.

Moreover, there were serious concerns over the simple practicalities of the arrival of thousands of soldiers in a rural area. Local services were just not up to the amount of work involved in such a large undertaking. The roads used to carry heavy materials into the camp were seriously damaged by such a huge increase in traffic. There were also worries over the sanitation facilities available at the camp, which were considered inadequate to cope with the numbers of men expected to arrive, and what if the new arrivals brought infectious diseases? Would the medical services in the area cope?

The new camp at Clipstone, which was to be the Sportsmen's new home.

By January, there were over 700 huts at the camp and it was large enough to hold over 12,000 men. Many more men were expected to arrive later. What had been unspoiled countryside was now covered in numerous wooden huts and rifle ranges. Instead of farmers ploughing the fields, soldiers were now digging trenches in them. The influx of men had a great influence on local towns, as trade for businesses more than doubled. The new arrivals also had a great effect on local ladies – not such a very popular development among the local men.

Not all the men from Clipstone Camp were successful in reaching the trenches of France. Twenty-eight of the camp's military occupants and a nurse are buried in the churchyard of St Albans in Forest Town. A number of those died of pneumonia. The camp eventually had its own hospital, which treated men who were wounded in France, as well as those from the camp who were taken ill. Some of the health problems at the camp resulted from the lack of a proper sewage system, which was not put into full operation until the following year.

One of the first units to arrive at the camp was the UPS Battalion in May 1915. There was a serious mix-up in the battalion's travel plans and many of the early occupants actually went to Clipstone, close to Market Harborough. Not everything at the camp was ready for early arrivals, as there was still no electricity and many of the huts leaked.

The University and Public Schools Battalion (UPS) began life at Epsom but were the first occupants of Clipstone Camp.

Most of the troops arriving at Clipstone left their trains at Edwinstowe Station and marched to the camp. It seems strange that they did not use the same route as their equipment, which was unloaded from the goods wagons that were run into sidings that had been built alongside the camp. There was no reason why the men could not have been driven into the sidings as well.

Although there had been around 5,000 members of the UPS, enough for four battalions at Epsom, as expected, the majority of these were given commissions into other regiments. The replacements were not all from public schools or universities, and later the character of the regiment dramatically changed. As with the Sportsmen at Hornchurch, the UPS also produced their own magazine, *Pow Wow*.

The first arrivals at Clipstone, original members of the UPS, found a fascinating pastime, which most of the men would have never experienced during their privileged upbringing. They went on visits to Mansfield Colliery and saw first hand what it was like for those who had to work underground. A more traditional recreation for men of their position was offered to them as well: membership to the Sherwood Golf Club.

The troops that arrived in the summer of 1915 found themselves in an enormous and incomplete camp. There was still plenty of work to do, such as the levelling of the parade grounds. Although the undergrowth had been mainly cleared from the site, it had in many places been piled in heaps and needed removal and burning. There was also a need for roads to be made throughout the camp. The feeling amongst most of the new arrivals was that they previously made themselves comfortable after a lot of hard work in the smaller camps and now had to start all over again. Along with the large number of wooden huts, a tented camp sprang up on nearby Walker's plantation. At this stage of the war, tented accommodation for soldiers was becoming much more common.

Councillor Hufton's fears about the moral and religious needs of the men seem to have been groundless, as the camp eventually contained one of the largest YMCA huts in the country. The 150ft x 40ft building included a 120ft concert room, four billiard tables, a library, and refreshments were available. While the hut was being completed, church services were provided in large marquees. The *Pow Wow* reported that for sixpence one could eat eggs, bread and butter, coffee and a cake at the YMCA. They also supplied the men with free writing paper, ink and pens. Many of the letters written by soldiers during the war were written on YMCA-headed notepaper.

Concerts were held at the camp on Thursday evenings, mainly performed by the people of Mansfield and often attended by the town's mayor. The concerts were performed by members of the battalions who had arrived at the camp. There was no shortage of talent within the ranks, especially after the Sportsmen arrived.

John Chessire had been aware of an expected move by the Sportsmen's Battalion from Hornchurch, by 21 June, but was still unsure of where they were going. He thought it was to be Ripon. Others in the battalion were evidently better informed, as they believed correctly that the destination was Nottingham.

The *Mansfield Chronicle* of 1 July 1915 reported that Clipstone had evidently become the rendezvous of the Royal Fusiliers, as in the preceding seven weeks, four battalions, which constituted the 99th Brigade of the Fusiliers, had been posted to the camp. There seems to have been a rapid rapport between the Fusiliers and the townspeople. This had been instigated by the early arrivals, who had endeavoured to put the locals' minds at rest as to the disruption the soldiers' arrival might have caused. The Sportsmen were to travel to London and march from Mark Lane to Marylebone, to join up with other battalions that made up the 99th Brigade. From there they were to travel by train to Clipstone Camp.

The men at Clipstone found themselves well cared for by the large number of nurses based there.

When the Sportsmen arrived at the camp there was much exploring to be done, including finding out the distance between the camp and Mansfield. Unfortunately, they found it to be nearly three miles to the town. The Sportsmen were to be part of the 99th Brigade, along with the 17th Empire Battalion, the 22nd Kensington's Battalion and the 24th Service Battalions Royal Fusiliers. The 24th was the 2nd Sportsmen's Battalion, which also came to Clipstone from Romford. The brigade training of the battalion at Clipstone consisted of more route marches in larger units, and the building of a rifle range. It was only after the rifle range was completed that they actually moved on to Tidworth.

In a letter John Chessire described his arrival at the camp. The battalion arrived at Mansfield but was not allowed to get off the train. It finally arrived at Edwinstowe and was allowed off for a very hot march to the camp. There were about 20,000 men already there, but with plans for a total of up to 80,000 at Clipstone. Nothing at the camp was ready for the Sportsmen as they were two weeks early. The men had to make their own beds by stuffing straw in bags. This seemed to be quite normal, however, as it happened at other camps as well. The camp post office was at the other end of the camp. This was a nuisance for such a prolific letter writer as John.

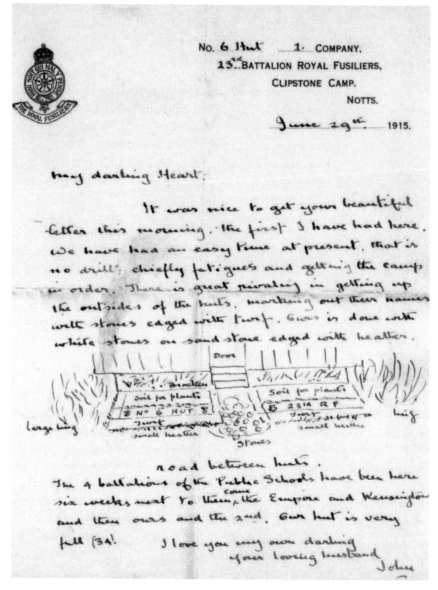

One of John Chessire's letters from Clipstone had a drawing showing his wife how the men had designed a garden outside the hut. (C. Chaloner)

Although an advance party of the Sportsmen arrived at Clipstone on a Friday, the main body arrived on Saturday to bring the strength of the two Sportsmen's battalions up to about 4,000. Those who left Hornchurch on that Friday had travelled on the Midland Railway, via Nottingham, where they stopped for refreshments. Those who travelled on that Saturday used the Great Eastern and Great Northern railways.

The area around Clipstone had been very dry, and dust was a big problem for the men on route marches. When the Sportsmen arrived at Edwinstowe from Hornchurch, the three-mile march from the station was marked by heavy rain, which settled the dust but seemed to have followed them from Hornchurch.

John described the outside of the huts as very plain. This led to a competition between the Sportsmen and other battalions to get them up to standard. John drew a picture on his letter of 29 June showing how the Sportsmen designed the gardens around the huts. There were no drills for a short period after they arrived. All their time was spent getting the camp in order.

The Sportsmen were posted to the far end of the camp, which was closest to Clipstone and a mile from the Mansfield end of the camp. The Sportsmen's part of the camp was described by a reporter in the *Mansfield Chronicle* as looking quite picturesque, the men taking pride in their lines. The Sportsmen had laid out rockeries and gardens round their huts, but owing to a shortage of plants they went outside the camp onto the common and dug up heather, which they then replanted around their gardens. The other units competing with the Sportsmen to upgrade their surroundings were the four battalions of the UPS, the Empire Battalion, the Kensington's and 2nd Battalion of the Sportsmen. Chessire was not impressed with all his competitors. The Empire men he describes as being very small, mostly of the city clerk type with pale faces.

The Sportsmen's Battalion was moved to Clipstone for brigade training, but rumours had been circulating at Grey Towers about the move for weeks before this move happened. Speculation grew about most of the objectives of the battalion through their time in England and in France. During their training at Clipstone the battalion was equipped with transport. Before long they were sent out on route marches through Sherwood Forest.

Coming together with other battalions awoke the competitive edge in John and the other men, in all areas, not just gardening. John described

how the Sportsmen's Battalion band was the best in the camp and drew crowds to listen every evening. The battalion also attracted a lot of attention in Mansfield, as they were led through the town by their band and their pipers. The noise of Scottish pipes brought the locals flocking out of their houses. They marched through two mining towns, Worksop and Mansfield Woodhouse, through very different surroundings than those they had grown used to at Hornchurch.

The Sportsmen were stationed at Clipstone during the camp's open day, when the public was allowed to see what was going on in what had been previously open countryside. Thousands of visitors turned up from the towns and villages surrounding the site. Friendships with the population of Mansfield grew close, just as they had with the people of Hornchurch.

Chessire described how there was still a large pool of recruits for the battalion at Hornchurch. Some of these were the men who had been left behind. John was still considering whether to ask for a commission. Colonel Maitland was refusing commissions for everyone at that time but once the new recruits from Hornchurch arrived, John hoped things would be different. It was also hard to get leave at that time because of the difficulty of getting a ticket on the railway, which was kept very busy with troop movements.

Garage (I.P)
Nottm. Quarters of the Road Club.

Black Boy Hotel,

Nottingham,

July 31ˢᵗ 1915.

TELEPHONES 3030. 3031

my darling Heart.

We have not yet got any thing in orders
about our move to Salisbury. a second
advance party left this morning. The
first party I understand found the
camp allotted to us "too far gone" to
do anything with. so instead of Bulford
it is to be Tidworth. and the date
probably Thursday. aug 5ᵗʰ. on
Tuesday next I understand we
shall start taking in rotation
4 days leave and 6 for long distances
25 % at a time. This afternoon I got
a nice letter from Colonel Colvin
(3ʳᵈ Essex Regiment Harwich) He says:-

Letters were not only sent from the camp but also from hostelries such as this hotel, sent when the men were on leave. (C. Chaloner)

Opposite: _It was not only Fusiliers at the camp, as this group of Royal Engineers shows._

John's next letter contained less hopeful news in relation to his promotion. Someone had offered to speak to the colonel of the 3rd Essex
about a commission for him but it seems there was a problem back in
Essex. The men of the 1st Battalion, who had been left at Hornchurch,
were moved to Gidea Park but because of the bad feeling about being
left behind there had been some riotous behaviour and several windows were broken. A number of the men were arrested. There were
no reports of this in the local Essex newspapers, so perhaps it was
felt it should not be publicised. The incident, however, seemed to
put an end to hopes of a commission for John. This report of trouble
back in Essex was also mentioned by another man, but according to
Private Ferrie, who was at Gidea Park at the time, most of the unrest
was due to the ages of the men. He described those left behind as
mainly men over forty years old, not allowed to make progress due
to their advanced age. He found this strange in a battalion which was
allowed to recruit men up to the age of forty-five. The men would not
be discharged as they were too useful for minor jobs, such as wash-
ing. Ferrie thought that the men would be used for nothing more
than home defence. This situation naturally led to bad feelings, which
often surfaced in heavy drinking. Ferrie related how he often locked
several men in the guardroom at Gidea Park due to drunkenness
while he was on guard duty.

The companies of the 1st Battalion left at Hornchurch joined with the
2nd Battalion men who had stayed on at Romford. For a time, it looked
as though they may have become the 3rd Battalion. The Sportsmen,
therefore, still had influence on events in the local Romford area, both
those who had left and those who had stayed. In August a case was
heard in Romford Court against Lieutenant Francis Gilbert Pearson,
of the 1st Battalion, who was charged with dangerous driving outside
Grey Towers Camp. The police officer that stopped him said that
he must have been travelling between 30 and 40mph. Pearson was
fined £5, with 10s cost for his absence because he had already left
Hornchurch with the battalion.

Clipstone Camp brought some level of prosperity to the local area.
The soldiers at the camp provided thousands of new customers for
local businesses. Shops found themselves run off their feet after being
accustomed to serving small village communities. Local families often
took in boarders from soldiers' families who were visiting their men at
the camp and local taxis had never been so busy.

One of John Chessire's inventions – a dog cart to carry a machine-gun. (C. Chaloner)

There must have been mixed feelings in the local community over the men at the camp, as in all communities where soldiers were posted. While the men at the camp seemed to be spending their time in safety and relative comfort, men from the local communities, who had joined up earlier in the war, were already abroad and in some cases were dying in France.

The following is a report from a newspaper entitled 'Brigade March of the Royal Fusiliers':

The 17th Empire, 22nd Kensington's and 23rd Sportsmen's Battalions of the Royal Fusiliers which with the 24th 2nd Sportsmen's form the 99th Infantry Brigade took part in a brigade march yesterday in fine weather. The 2nd Sportsmen's were unable to take part owing to so many of them being engaged on battalion fatigues.

The Kensington's led the way followed by the Sportsmen's and the Empire. They marched from the camp, along Mansfield Road to Clipstone Drive then through Mansfield Woodhouse. They then went via Market Warsop, Warsop Hill and back to Clipstone. The men accompanied by their bands aroused a lot of public attention in Mansfield Woodhouse and Worsop. Many of the Sportsmen later had a bath in the Vicar Water.

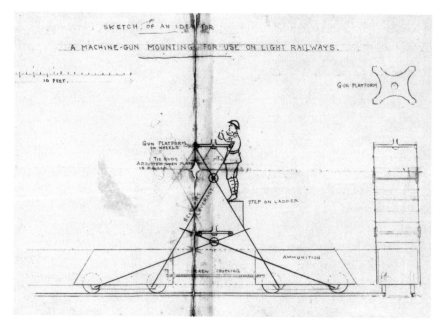

John Chessire was very inventive, as well as being a talented artist, as this machine-gun mounting for protecting light railways shows. (C. Chaloner)

The 1st Sportsmen's and the Empire bands gave a public performance a few days later on the parade ground at the camp. The 2nd Sportsmen's arranged an athletics meeting at the Forest Town Institute. Soldiers in uniform were admitted free but civilians had to pay. The 2nd battalion organised a similar event just before leaving Hare Hall but this had to be cancelled due to their leaving for Clipstone.

The Sportsmen went to Clipstone in June 1915 and stayed until they moved on to Tidworth Camp, on Salisbury Plain. In John Chessire's letter of 22 July he said that they were to move to Salisbury Plain within a few days. This development would finally put an end to his hopes of a commission. But the rumours were not true and he was still at Clipstone at the end of the month. In fact, the battalion was then told they would be leaving by 3 August and that they would be in France by 17 September. John was informed about this by a member of the Army Service Corps. The battalion received new uniforms before leaving Clipstone.

John described how they underwent fighting practice in Sherwood Forest, which would have been pleasant if it had not been so wet. He was also very pleased with the church parades at Clipstone, and the band who played the music for the hymns. Colonel Winter had private rooms in Forest Town, so it seems that senior officers did not have to reside at the camp.

Two advance parties left for Salisbury and found the camp they had been allocated too far gone, so they were moved to Tidworth. John Chessire had received a letter from the colonel of the 3rd Essex, in Harwich, who wanted to meet him to speak about his application for a commission. The colonel said that he preferred to meet candidates for commissions personally, but as they had attended the same school, he would send him a form to fill in if he could not get leave.

Clipstone Camp continued to be used throughout the war and was also utilised as a demobilisation point after the war. The presence of so many soldiers, for such a long period, obviously had a great effect in the area.

CHAPTER 7

THE BATTALION AT TIDWORTH

Researching Tidworth in the First World War was challenging. There are several military postcards from the period that place Tidworth in Wiltshire, while others place it in Hampshire. They both turned out to be correct. North Tidworth has always been in Wiltshire. South Tidworth was in Hampshire until 1992, when it was transferred to Wiltshire. The Tidworth Camp was, until then, spread across two counties. Both villages had already become united by the Army camps that had sprung up in the area since the end of the nineteenth century, despite being in different counties. Salisbury Plain had been selected by the Army as an ideal site for military manoeuvres in the mid-nineteenth century. There were few farms and inhabitants to interfere with military matters and at the time no nearby military camps where the soldiers on manoeuvres could be billeted. The military had already taken over much of the local area as a training ground before they began to plan permanent camps.

The Government bought around 40,000 acres of land in the area, which included the estate of Sir John Kelk, in Tedworth. Although the sale was completed by 1897, it was not until the early years of the twentieth century that serious work began on turning the site into a large military camp. There were plans to sell existing buildings on the site, such as Tedworth House, but this never happened. The camp became a garrison attached to the Southern Military Command. Tedworth House was then used as the home of the officer in command, instead of being sold.

The camp at Tidworth was in a remote area as this postcard shows, but was different from what the Sportsmen had so far experienced.

The early years of the twentieth century were spent erecting numerous new buildings and providing the necessary services for the planned large military presence. By the time the First World War began there was an isolation hospital in Brimstone Bottom, built in 1900, sewerage works at Tidworth Park in 1903, and even an Army extension from the Midland and South Western Junction Railway, at Ludgershall, since 1901. The first troops at the camp were housed in tents or wooden huts until brick barracks were built later.

A military cemetery was added in 1904, interestingly enough three years before the military hospital was built. The Lucknow and Mooltan barracks were built in 1905, and Tin Town was erected about the same time at Brimstone Bottom to provide huts and recreation buildings for labourers who were working on the building of the barracks. New roads were also laid by the Army, a theatre opened and a garrison power station began generating in 1914, which made an electric cinema possible. The barracks were built with four infantry barrack buildings in the centre, with cavalry barracks on its flanks. This reflected the positioning of the troops at the battle of Marston Moor, the last battle to be fought on British soil. The barracks themselves were named after places in India and Afghanistan, where many of the first soldiers were stationed.

110

CANDAHAR, TIDWORTH.   4688

The brick-built barracks gave the impression of the camp being a town.

When the troops began to arrive at the outset of the First World War, many would have been there before. Tidworth had been used for summer camps for boys from the public schools' officer training corps. Some of the Sportsmen's Battalion and a number of the UPS Battalion had been members of these groups.

The First World War brought a more sombre look to the camp. Before the war, the regiments based there had worn colourful uniforms, often with bright metal helmets or bearskin. Church parades on Sundays had become a tourist attraction, with visitors eager to see the men in their fine coloured dress. However, those thousands of arrivals for war service were clad in drab khaki, which did not give the same romantic impression.

There were irritating difficulties and discomforts to contend with at the camp from early on in the war. One soldier wrote in November 1914 that icy mud flowed over the floor up to 2in deep. Tent pegs lost their hold and tents collapsed causing everything inside the tents, including bedding, clothes and men to become covered in mud. When one considers the size of the camp at Tidworth it shows how inadequate the camps were for the actual numbers involved in the recruits for war. The large brick barracks did not provide enough space for the men and tented camps sprang up around the area.

Tidworth House was used by officers as a club.

When Private Worger, of the 2nd Sportsmen's Battalion, arrived at Tidworth, he was not impressed. He was told by some of the men there who had already been at the front that if they could stand Tidworth they could stand anything. Worger was finding it difficult to deal with the training, perhaps due to his age of over forty. During a route march, one of his friends offered to carry his rifle. He told the man that if he could not carry his own rifle while training he would be no good at the job. Worger must have come late from Romford and missed out on the time at Clipstone because he thought the training at Tidworth was much harder than it had been at Gidea Park, which tailed off towards the end. Private Worger also mentioned that there were plans for the battalion to be reviewed by Queen Mary while they were at Tidworth.

Another hutted camp was built in 1915, as well as new tented ones to provide extra accommodation for troops for the war. Tedworth House had by that time become an officers' club. An ordnance depot was also added to the site during the war. By the time the Sportsmen's Battalion arrived Tidworth had become a large military town, with a military school and church. Not only British soldiers were based at the vastly expanded camp; Canadians arrived from very early in the

John Chessire found the brick-built accommodation rather like a prison.

war. Australians came later, as did a small number of New Zealanders. Many of these troops from across the world remained permanently at the camp. Around 150 Australians and 100 New Zealanders are buried in the camp cemetery.

The journey from Clipstone Camp for the Sportsmen was far from straightforward. The route took them through Leicester, Rugby, Banbury, Reading and Newbury. They were given bread and butter and coffee at Banbury by the Red Cross. They arrived at Tidworth at 7.30 p.m. and once again had to make their own beds using straw and bags. Chessire said that the Warwicks had left the barracks in a poor state, probably because they had only received four hours' notice before the move. John described the brick barracks as a great change from huts but not entirely an improvement: they were more like a prison, with rooms built for twelve men but holding nineteen.

Tidworth was a regular camp, with proper streets of houses for married servicemen, telegraph poles and brick-built barracks, unlike the temporary camps the Sportsmen had been in until then. The first day after the battalion arrived was spent cleaning their new homes. The whole 99th Brigade went to Tidworth and became part of the 33rd Division, with its double three domino insignia.

Tidworth had married quarters but not for the wives of the new army, only regulars.

Church parade was held in the theatre, which was big enough to hold around 2,000 men and considered by John to be very stuffy. As well as infantry, there were around 10,000 cavalry in the barracks, including Dragoons and the 10th Hussars. The artillery was based at Bulford. John would often walk there to see what it was like.

Although it is common knowledge that lice were a great problem for the men in the trenches in France, they were also a problem in the camps at home. John Chessire mentions cutting them down with paraffin while at Tidworth.

John was missing his wife by this time. He mentioned how good it was to think that she was only two hours away at Cheltenham, close enough to send him hard-boiled eggs. This must have helped, for the food at Tidworth was poor due to the overcrowded conditions. The bread he described as the sort that absorbed all the bad atmosphere.

It was becoming obvious by the end of August that there was little chance of the battalion reaching France any time soon, and surely not by the date they were previously given, in September. Although long leaves had been cancelled, which seemed to point to movement soon, the 33rd Division still had no artillery. The battalion was then moved from the brick barracks into tents, after the arrival of even more men, thus making it clear that they were not going to move in the near future.

There were already trenches at Tidworth, so the battalion did not have to dig them. During trench training, one platoon of the battalion got lost and sat in the trench waiting for their officer to come and get them. It turned out that he had gone home. Chessire said it was not the first time that this officer had left them in the lurch, which did not inspire much hope for their time in France. Brigade route marches now included transport wagons, drawn by mules and horses from Canada.

There was a great deal of practice in moving as a brigade. The battalion was used as a rearguard on one occasion, and on another march they took artillery, cavalry and field kitchens with them – though no hot drinks, despite the kitchens.

There was bad news for John from Harwich. The War Office would not sanction any more changes in the division, so his hopes of a commission were dashed. However, he did get a new rifle which he was very pleased with, apart from its stiff bolt. Two of the company's new rifles broke on the first day because they were made so quickly, no surprise when one considers how many were needed. Having new rifles was quite a luxury that early in the war. Many units were forced to use inferior *Ross*, *Arisaka* or *Long Lee-Enfield* rifles because the more modern *Short Magazine Lee-Enfield* rifle was in short supply. Introduced in 1902, this rifle was 'short' because of the length of the gun, not its magazine. It was easily distinguished from the single-shot *Lee-Enfield* rifle of the previous century. The newer version held ten rounds in its magazine. Some believed that there was so much emphasis on bayonet practice during training because it was easier to organise and did not use vital ammunition, such as in firing practice. When one considers how much actual bayonet fighting took place in the war compared to the amount of firing, then perhaps there is something to this view.

The position of the camp was seven miles to Andover and fourteen to Marlboro and Salisbury. John Chessire commented that really one needed a car in a place like that. There were apparently less visits to the local area, as trips out were rarely mentioned in John's letters. One exception was a trip to Salisbury to meet his brother Cecil, where he found the Red Lion Hotel full of officers, and the White Hart was even worse. This seems to point to the fact that officers were better able to get out of camp than privates. In a later letter, he mentioned that he was supposed to meet his brother again but could not get a pass to get out of camp.

The church at Tidworth was a favourite place for John Chessire.

During brigade bivouacs, many of the men provided their own refreshments. John describes how that one night they slept in a beech wood with an undergrowth of nut trees. They were not provided with blankets until 2.00 a.m., and the soup they were given was so bad that they threw it away. However, they brought their own cocoa and also had meat and gingerbread cakes. John did not think that the general wanted them to have much food during the exercise, perhaps as practice for facing shortages later in France.

The next brigade march and bivouac lasted for three days. The march was always tedious due to hold ups resulting from blockages on the road, inevitable when there were such large numbers of men and equipment involved. There were observers who would follow the route 200 yards away from the road. At night it was easy for these observers to get lost in the dark.

A battalion letter, dated 16 September, from the Orderly Room at Tidworth explained that training for the week ending 18 September would be at Wick Down. It seems that there was a change from one company to a small unit, acting as an attacking force.

The only way for those serving in the Army to see their wives or girlfriends was to meet while they had leave in a nearby town. It had become very difficult for John to get home, but his wife did come to Malboro to meet him on a number of occasions.

The trench practice at the end of October was good preparation for France. Continual rain meant that the men were again digging trenches in wet soil. Some of the men fell into the 6ft-deep trenches. All of their equipment, including rifles, was invariably covered in mud and had to be cleaned every evening before bedtime.

There was a touching letter from John to his daughter Deborah in October, for her fifth birthday. He sent her a shilling to buy a present and hoped she had a cake with five candles. Being separated from family must have been one of the hardest things for married men to bear.

There was a change of mood in the next letter, as John described bomb practice. The bombs they used were made from iron cylinders filled with gunpowder and with each end packed with clay. There was a timed fuse that was lit as the bomb was thrown. One man in C Company dropped a bomb at his feet and everyone around him ran for cover before the bomb blew up. The type of bombs used during the war developed throughout the conflict. The type being used by the battalion must have been quite advanced. Some of the earlier types were made from old jam tins. John also mentioned how they had to wear their overcoats and packs because they could soon be leaving for France.

In October, John wrote a long essay about railways and home defence. He believed that the ability to repel foreign invasion of England rested on rapid mobilisation of home troops. This depended on the railway system, which was fine for troops travelling from north to south, but was lacking in allowing movement from east to west. The problem was that there was no direct railway line between Worcester and Warwick. John's idea to remedy this was a military road between these points, with military bases at each point where the railway crossed it. Troops could then transfer from one mode of transport to another. He lists these planned military depots as Worcester, Warwick, Rugby and Market Harborough – ideal spots for cavalry because they were centres of hunting. Warwick was also the centre of the automobile industry and so could supply motor transport for troops to move them along the road to rail points. This project would have improved the ability of the Army to quickly move to any area threatened with invasion. Construction of the road would also provide useful employment for those men without work.

Letters were no longer written on battalion-headed notepaper but were now, like so many other First World War letters, on paper supplied by the YMCA. (C. Chaloner)

John's letter of 12 November made it clear that the battalion was finally on their way to France. The address of the battalion was written on the bottom of the letter. The king's message had been read out to them that morning, as it was to every soldier going abroad. John wrote that the position of the battalion would be near to one of the scenes from the book *The Three Musketeers*. He was considering asking someone to get him some French money in London, as there would be a better exchange rate there than in France. He mentioned how his five-year-old daughter would be frightened by his gas helmet. It must have frightened many of the men who had to wear it.

There was a delay for the battalion on 14 November. The 30th Division, which was in front of them trying to cross into France, was held up at Folkestone because of bad weather. For the first time there is a joke in one of John's letters, perhaps a sign of frayed nerves. Referring to the bad language of the men, he said that the mules, which were kept in sheds at the rear of the tents, should not have to put up with such rude men. John also explained to his wife how his letters from the front would be censored, and wondered if the censor would know what 'ILY' meant.

The first of the battalion to leave Tidworth was an advance party of four officers and 122 men. Afterwards, a second group left consisting of twelve officers and 433 men.

CHAPTER 8

AND SO TO FRANCE

On 16 November 1915, the battalion travelled from Tidworth to Folkestone and then made the crossing to Boulonge, which they reached on 17 November. Their first port of call was Ostrohove K Rest Camp, which they did not reach until midnight. The total strength of the battalion was twenty-six officers and 871 other ranks. Any rest they managed at Ostrohove was short-lived as the next day they boarded trains at Pont De Brigues for Steenbecque, where they were billeted in barns and farmhouses, which was to be the norm for much of the war. They were finally close enough to the front to hear the sound of gunfire.

The 2nd Battalion had also crossed into France. Private Worger described the crossing as good, but not so good was the forty-eight hours spent in a camp in France, with twelve men to a tent in a sea of mud. This was probably the same camp that the 1st Battalion stayed in, as John Chessire was similarly derogatory about it. Private Worger also found the twenty-four hours in a cattle truck quite unpleasant.

Chessire's first letter from France seemed to have a more sombre tone than his previous ones, which had been written back in England. He had a good journey but it was slow. As they were not staying where they were, there was no need for him to explain to his wife how many slept in a tent or whether, because he was tall, his feet were able to fit in it. He described the barn in which they were resting, but really all he wanted was a good pair of boots. When arriving in France, he found out the meaning of wet feet, blaming the Army's issue of overseas boots, which were of no use at all. Complaints about Army issue equipment were nothing new.

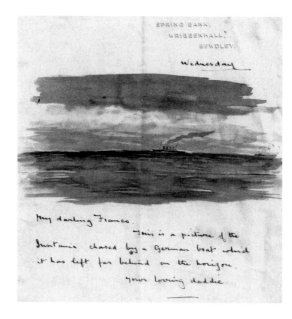

Left: *One of John's paintings of the* Lusitania, *sent to his daughter Frances.*
(C. Chaloner)

Opposite: *A famous green envelope. Letters in these were not censored at regimental level.*
(C. Chaloner)

The address that letters were to be sent to in reply had also changed. Instead of the 33rd Division, they were supposed to be sent to the Right Flank Company. Moreover, they were no longer allowed to mention what they were doing or where they were.

On 23 November, the battalion marched to Busnes, where the men were paid. As they moved closer to the front the landscape changed for the worse, with most of the houses in ruins. In the same month, the 99th Brigade was transferred to the 2nd Division in exchange for the 19th Brigade. The 1st Sportsmen's Battalion was also separated from the 2nd Battalion, which was replaced in the 99th Brigade by the King's Royal Rifle Corps.

Major General Pereria had no experience of the new Army units and the Sportsmen came as a pleasant surprise to him. He found that the men had the same spirit and self-confidence as he had seen among regular soldiers with a regimental history to help form them into a unit.

The area of Bethune was an important centre behind the British front line. It was a billeting town with a railway junction and a hospital. In 1915 Robert Graves wrote a poem about watching the seasons pass in Bethune, called 'Fairies and Fusiliers'. Between Bethune and Cambrian was Woburn Abbey Military Cemetery. It was begun by the Royal

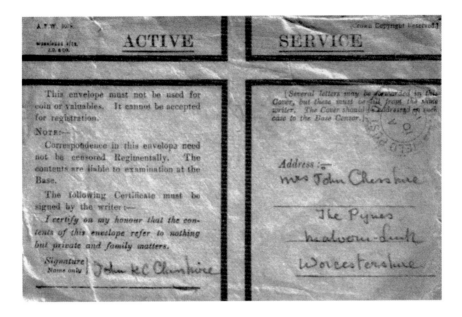

Berkshire Regiment in June 1915, but it was closed in the following years because it was so exposed to enemy action.

It was during November that John Chessire sent his first letter in a green envelope. A green envelope was not censored regimentally. The envelope had to be signed by the sender to swear on his honour that the letter enclosed would only refer to private and family matters. John seemed to be over his first bad impressions of the country and to have become used to his wet feet. They all were very warm in their barn and liked where they were based. He could say he loved Dorothy as many times as he liked in this letter, safe in the knowledge it was in the green envelope.

The first experience that the men had in the trenches was a gradual acclimatisation to the front line. Small groups were placed with regular, more experienced troops in the line so that they could learn what was expected. The battalion was allocated to the 6th Infantry Division for trench training. It was while members of the battalion were involved in working parties at the front that the first casualty was suffered when one man was slightly wounded. One of the more serious incidents involved members of the Right Flank Company who were caught by shrapnel while walking along a road, when ten men and NCOs were wounded. This gradual familiarisation to the front seemed to be the way most new units were introduced to the trenches. The men of the

10th Essex reported a similar introduction – the only difference was that they were shelled while making their first visit. They initially described it as a very heavy bombardment but were soon corrected by the more experienced men who said it was just light shelling.

The trauma of what happened in the trenches was too much for some men, though I did not find a record of any case of shell shock amongst the Sportsmen. There were different ways of treating those who could not take the strain of the front line. For some, the shock of warfare was too much and they ran. The debate still rages over how these men were treated. Some of the men who suffered from shell shock and absconded were treated as deserters and shot. The number of men who were executed in the British Army ran into the hundreds. Whether this helped to instil discipline is doubtful. In the Italian Army, the death sentences ran into the thousands, although not all were carried out, and their discipline was generally much poorer than that of the British Army. The German Army, however, had far lighter penalties for offences and discipline was enforced more gently.

Siegfried Sassoon described how if a man became a dud in the ranks, he stayed there until he was killed or wounded. If an officer became a dud, he was found a soft job at base. There appears to have been different rules for officers when it came to having difficulty coping. It was likely that seeing an officer with such problems was considered bad for morale. It would not sit well with the image that these fine young men portrayed.

Private Worger, of the 2nd Battalion, was also experiencing trench warfare for the first time. He told his wife in a letter that she could believe all that was said about the trenches. It was impossible to exaggerate the terrible conditions they found themselves in.

The reason that so much of the land was in such a terrible condition was the shelling. Areas like the region around Ypres were originally marsh land that had over time been drained by the use of canals and dykes. Despite warnings from locals British shelling in the area destroyed the drainage system, which led to flooding and deep mud. In winter, this became even worse with heavy rain. The German trenches were mainly on higher and therefore drier ground, which meant that their positions were far more pleasant and consequently healthier.

Private Worger wrote the title 'Somewhere in France' on his letters. He described the scene as a land of mud and misery. Four days in a trench was almost bearable, but the worst thing about it was the lack of sleep while at the front. The new men were given tips on how to

A German postcard with a map showing some of the locations that were to become so well known to many of the British Army arriving on the continent.

survive by a man he described as an 'unshaved soldier'. Worger was to quickly experience at first hand the dangers of war when a piece of shrapnel hit him in the foot. Fortunately it was spent before it reached him. Others were not so lucky. The 2nd Battalion suffered their first fatality on their second day in the trenches. Worger described how a man was killed instantly and said he was at least thankful it had been quick.

The 1st Battalion's first experience of trench warfare was in the town of Cambrin. The brigade's headquarters was located in this town, less than 1,000 yards from the front line. It was close to the site of the Battle of Loos, which took place between September and October, before the battalion arrived. The Battle of Loos was the first occasion that British troops used poisonous gas. It had also been the first big push of the war and included six divisions, many of them with no experience of conflict.

Despite the restrictions of the earlier letter to his wife, in which he was not permitted to say what they were doing, John sent a good description of the battalion's first experience of the front line. They marched up Cambrian Road on a foul night. It was pouring with rain and pitch dark. They were overdressed for a working party – it was the

123

Drawing and painting materials were scarce at the front. John explains that the drawing was spoilt by his purple pencil. (C. Chaloner)

first and last time they wore overcoats in the trenches. John said that it was worse than going to a dance in full dress uniform, where dinner jackets were required. By the time they reached the communication trench, every square inch of their coats had absorbed their full ration of water. That was one thing that the men who trained them had forgotten to mention.

It took about an hour to walk the half mile in the communication trench because of the darkness and mud. The trench was a putty-coloured clay, varying in depth from 6–7ft – as John describes, as wide as a large coffin. It was wide enough to get a grip on the sides with both elbows and it was on this that they depended for support. The walking was so hard that they did not notice the sound of the guns. They were happy for the star shells that infrequently gave light.

The task the Sportsmen were given was to build up a parapet within about forty yards of the German trenches. Despite the stress of their

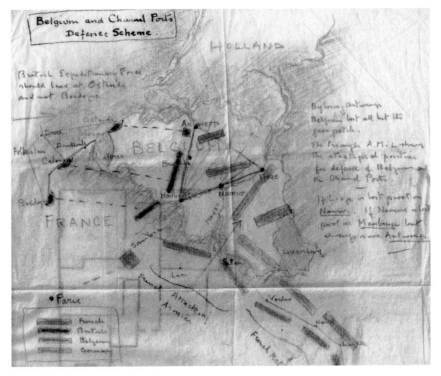

More of John Chessire's strategies and plans for the war. (C. Chaloner)

new surroundings, John included some jokes in his letters. He said that they went to church parade armed to the teeth, but were allowed to take the knives out of their mouths to sing hymns. He also said that they had their first bath in France in a coal mine, and needed to wash afterwards.

John later gave a fuller account of what trench life was really like – endless halts as they progressed through the trenches, sometimes every fifty yards or so. Once it got dark, it was hard to stay awake and he wondered how he was going to face four days in the trenches, which was the duration of the average spell. The last hours of the march were over horrible marshes and shell holes, and much of it across greasy planks crossing streams in single file.

The hardest time to keep awake in the trenches was just before day-break. John once fell off the firing step at 5.00 a.m., after about two seconds of sleep. This would have been sufficient reason for him to be shot at dawn but luckily no one noticed. Falling asleep on duty was common and there were numerous courts-martial for it, resulting in the handing out of hundreds of death sentences, though relatively few of these sentences were carried out. When one considers how many soldiers there were and how very tired they must have been, the numbers charged seem surprisingly low.

Just before daybreak was one of the two supposed danger periods in the front line. It was not a good time to fall asleep. This was when the men would 'Stand to Arms', standing ready with their rifles. This duty lasted an hour and was repeated at dusk, during the dangerous half-light.

The battalion was in the front line with the 7th Berkshires and 5th Liverpool. There was an increase in casualties as they went into December, although many of these were accidental injuries which occurred while they were involved in working parties. They also had to dig new trenches and experienced their first sight of aeroplanes at war. John Chessire described how fascinating it was to see the explosions of gunfire around the flying aircraft. One plane had about fifty shots aimed at it but still flew away unharmed. This must have been a novel sight for the men in the trenches as aircraft had only just begun to be utilised in warfare, but by the end of the war they were used much more.

The roads were bad near the front, thick with mud and badly dug out by the transports. He told his wife about a small church nearby that had been badly knocked about by artillery, and how eight carved figures were taken out and stored in a nearby cellar for safekeeping. The destruction of a church must have had a sad effect on John.

Many of the items needed in the trenches could be bought in places like the Army and Navy Stores. Unfortunately many of those who served did not know what they needed until after they had been in the trenches. Many officers bought their own wire cutters, which were better than Army issue, and even their own automatic pistols. Mortleman's Patent Sound Absorbers were also available, which were earplugs designed to cut out noise of the guns, but it is not clear how popular they were.

The 1st Battalion's first fatality was suffered on 5 December when a man was killed by shelling. On 7 December, Privates Ashwell and Clarke, a machine-gun crew, were killed by a shell. The numbers of deaths and injuries increased as the month progressed and the

The ruined buildings of the front shocked the men arriving from England. Destroyed churches seemed to have a great effect on John Chessire.

battalion began to take a more active role in the front line. Although conditions at the front were mainly kept from the population back home, it still seemed strange that so many men were shocked by what was happening. Anyone who had joined the Army must have realised that men would die at the front. Although it may have been hard to visualise how terrible some of those deaths might be, surely the recruits did not expect all deaths to be painless and noble. Charles Edmonds described how the horror of the front affected him. He said that he could never get the memory of the battles out of his mental system. He claimed he was not disillusioned by the experience. Perhaps, then, some of those more prolific men who were traumatised and who subsequently wrote about their experiences had entered into battle with romantic and unrealistic impressions of modern warfare.

John received a letter from his Aunt Addie. She hoped that he was comfortable in his new surroundings. He thought that at any moment they would have to leave their dugout, due to the water that was seeping through the ceiling. It was not only dugouts that leaked – no house in the area had a roof or windows. However, it was the rats that bothered John the most. Moreover, the trenches offered little warmth.

Crosses from graves were burnt as firewood, but fires were rare due to a lack of fuel, and consequently food and drink were often served cold.

Despite the lack of hot food, and even drinking water, letters always seemed to reach the men. By 1918, the Army Postal Service employed 4,000 men. It only took two or three days for a letter to reach the Western Front from Britain. The men were still allowed a letter a day. What they wrote in reply was censored by officers, so the worst horrors of the war were kept from folk back home. There were cases when some details did get through, especially those mentioning how the men often stood in water up to their waists in the trenches. The Government passed the Defence of the Realm Act in 1914, which gave them the power to suppress published criticism of the war and imprison those responsible without trial. It is a strange concept that they wanted to suppress free speech when the British Army was supposedly fighting for freedom. The War Office Press Bureau censored newspaper reports in the same way that officers censored letters.

Although the men had gone through months of training in England, it was continued at the front. This meant that rest periods out of the front line were not restful at all. Gas training involved wearing a gas helmet and passing through a hut full of chlorine gas. John Chessire mentions the gas training, but only to say that they tried out their helmets. They also had lessons in avoiding frostbite.

It was not until 19 December that the battalion finally took over a section of the trenches at Cambrin, relieving the Royal Berks. The gas training would have been very useful, as a gas attack was ordered while the battalion was part of the front line, but this was cancelled due to the wind dropping. On 21 December, while on the front line at New Crater, a danger spot for snipers, a gas attack did take place. At times the mud in the trenches was above the men's knees and they were often driven out of the dugouts by the water leaking through the roof.

Rest periods out of the trenches often meant fatigues. John tried to describe life in the trenches but found it hard to do so without mentioning military matters. They stood in water night and day but he did not explain how this felt. Not mentioning casualties, he did say that the battalion had been through a fair sample of modern warfare, which doubtless included some unpleasant events. They had also been given leather sleeveless coats, which seemed to have been more popular with the troops than greatcoats.

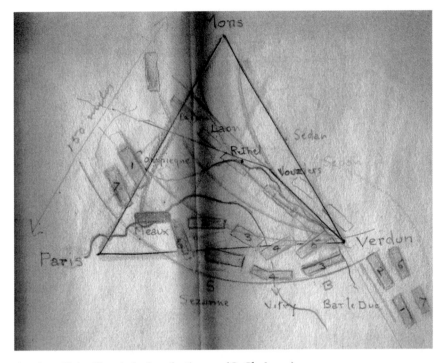

Another of John Chessire's plans for the war. (C. Chaloner)

There were regular periods of broken rest when the battalion was relieved from the line. Their first rest spell at the front lasted only a few days. When the Royal Berks moved back up on 22 December the Sportsmen moved back to Annequin, where there was very little in the way of comfort; there was no material for fires or even straw to sleep on.

The battalion spent some time in a girls' school but there were 150 men in a room. John managed to get a hold of some rat poison but could not use it in the trenches as the rats were too numerous, often running over the rifles that were resting on the parapet. He evidently suffered from a wound, saying he had not kept any souvenirs of shell splinters, not even the piece that caught him on the thumb. The mud was a continual problem in the trenches, but John did not mention the exact depth of it in case it deterred would-be recruits.

The rest period before Christmas Day was not a pleasant one. They had no shelter and the only sleep they got was while standing up, like horses in a field. By Christmas Day they were back in the trenches,

John Chessire sent this small card in one of his letters, but it is not clear whether he produced the artwork himself. (C. Chaloner)

facing an artillery bombardment. It was also the battalion's first patrol, with five men heading over the top into No Man's Land. Patrols and raids were far more common than large attacks. Raids were often ordered to capture prisoners, so that knowledge of which enemy units they were facing in the trenches could be determined. Many of the men who took part in these raids believed that those in command ordered them because they thought that the raids would make them more aggressive, rather than for any real interest in prisoners. The battalion's patrol located a sniper's post and cut some wire from the enemy's defences while being shot at.

As Christmas Day approached there were fears amongst the top brass that there could be a repeat of the famous fraternisation which occurred the previous year between the British and German troops on Christmas Day. An order was sent to the battalion informing all ranks that any attempts at fraternisation with the enemy during Christmas or the New Year would be met with hostile action, and disobedience would lead to court martial. In other words, any German who got out of his trench to make friends or start a truce was to be shot on sight.

There was little Christmas cheer when on Boxing Day Colonel Maitland was wounded in the leg. The battalion spent five days on the line, with several casualties. Chessire said that five days in the trenches was about the limit of what they could stand. Most of the men had no shelter and hardly any sleep while at the front. It is hard to imagine how they could sleep in trenches that were over a foot deep in mud. A case was even reported of a sergeant major who drank Bovril (a trademark of concentrated beef extract) made with liquid gas which was stored in petrol tins, like the drinking water. An order was later passed to the front stating that all gas cylinders, both full and empty, were to be removed from the front line and stored at Cambrin Church – one that John would probably have found quite objectionable.

The battalion was next relieved by the 18th Royal Fusiliers on 29 December, and they moved back to Busnettes for sixteen days of rest. John Chessire described the billets as the best yet, and said that it was a great relief to be out of the range of gun noise. There was also a message delivered for Lieutenant Jourdain from the brigadier when they moved back from the front, congratulating him on his work during a patrol.

What had begun in the peace and tranquillity of Essex for the Sportsmen's Battalion in 1915 had moved them through camps in different parts of England, until they arrived in France. They finally embarked on the thing for which they had been training all this time: action.

CHAPTER 9

1916

The beginning of the New Year started peacefully for the battalion, as they were still at rest in Busnettes. Rest did not consist of long days relaxing in their billets. John Chessire's letter, again in a green envelope and dated 2 January, said that they were having a hard time and that he might be able to tell of his experiences in one of his other letters. There was still a constant round of kit inspections, drills and route marches for the battalion.

In his next letter, John thanked his wife for the new boots she had sent. The Army issue ones were useless for keeping the soldiers' feet dry and anyone who had their own pairs were allowed to wear them in the trenches but still had to wear the Army issue boots on route marches. There were some attempts at helping the men to deal with the mud. The battalion diaries spoke of how gumboots were to be handed back in when coming out of the trenches. They must have been issued when going into the front line and returned when relieved.

There was an exchange between 7 and 11 January of men amongst the Sportsmen and another battalion, which included officers and NCOs. This involved two company commanders, two subalterns, four sergeants and four corporals. They were exchanged on a temporary basis for similar ranks with the King's Royal Rifle Corps. According to the battalion diaries it was hoped they would learn many useful lessons from this, but no mention was made concerning what these lessons might have been.

By 11 January, there was leave for the officers, and by 19 January the battalion was back on duty at Le Touret, relieving the 6th Queens Regiment.

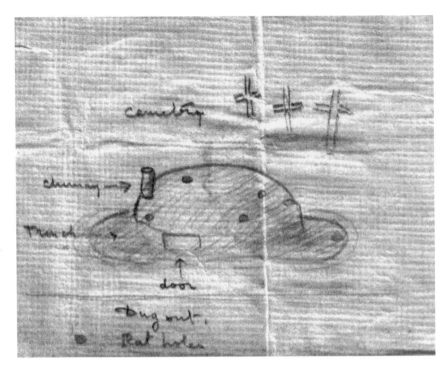

A drawing of a dugout by John Chessire. Note the rat holes: John was not very fond of rats. (C. Chaloner)

John had written how they would soon be back in the trenches. He hoped that they would not strike as rough a patch as the last time. He did not explain what this rough patch was, except to say that it was too full of incident to be pleasant. On 14 January, the 99th Infantry Brigade took over Section C of the front at Festubert from the 37th Infantry Brigade.

The battalion diary mentioned that the men were warned to be careful during the early part of the year, especially at Windy Corner in Festubert, which was an important shelter for the reserves. Every effort was to be made not to draw shellfire. The men were informed that they should not expose themselves during the day and that no vehicles were to move through the area during daylight hours.

On 27 January, the reserve troops were warned to 'Stand to Arms' in case of a possible enemy attack. All reserves had to be ready to move within an hour and a half. Sapping and machine-gun sections were instructed to rejoin their battalions. There was a lecture on the nature of the attack before they went back to the trenches. John, the master of understatement, said that going over the top did not sound inviting. He told his wife, Dorothy, of how they were gassed in their first venture into the trenches and described how it felt: 'It is so difficult groping around with your bayonet fixed and holding the rifle in one hand while keeping the eyeholes of the gas helmet positioned so you can see. Gas is a wicked form of warfare'. This was one of the earlier incidents he had referred to when explaining how bad their front line experience had been.

A number of the members of the battalion were taken by motor vehicle to level a nearby aerodrome, using slag from a local coalmine. John mentioned the French civilians for the first time, saying that two Frenchmen speaking make more noise than a brigade of Englishmen. 'It makes you hope that the population of France is small,' he said. The peculiarities of certain trenches were also mentioned, as those that are very close to the German lines were less likely to be shelled but were more prone to mines.

The battalion's postings seemed to be following the route of old battles. Festubert had been the scene of a battle the previous year. In May 1915, British, Canadian and Indian soldiers captured the village of Festubert, but the advance only measured around a kilometre at the expense of 16,000 casualties. The Canadians had problems with their standard issue *Ross* rifles then and none of the units had sufficient numbers of machine-guns. Shortages of equipment in the battle became public knowledge back home and aided the downfall of the Asquith Government and the formation of a coalition.

The battalion's trenches at that time could only be reached by going over the top. This meant that any movement had to be carried out at night. The battalion was supposed to be relieved by 27 January but there was rumoured to be a threat of attack, so they had to stay longer. In the event the attack never materialised, and the next day they were relieved and marched back to Bethune. By the end of the month, Colonel Maitland gave up command of the battalion, and Major Richey took over temporary command. The end of the month also saw the battalion at a division church parade attended by the corps commander. The next day, Lieutenant Colonel H. Vernon, previously of the Kings Royal Rifle Corps, assumed command of the battalion. Lieutenant Cooper was appointed machine-gun officer and Major Richey left to go on leave until 10 February.

Another of John's pictures but with no explanation. (C. Chaloner)

The new commander, Colonel Vernon, was mentioned by John Chessire in one of his letters, saying that Vernon was placed in the battalion under a new regime. John did not know if it was Scottish, French or Church law. It seems that the men were unsure of the new commander. Every man in the battalion over forty years of age was paraded and asked how they liked trench life. John's only comment on life on the front line was that he found it chilly. Whether this survey was entirely due to the presence of the new commander is unclear, but it is interesting that it happened at this time.

In early February the battalion moved to Le Quesnoy and again relieved the Royal Berks. The early months of the Sportsmen's war was spent in short periods in the trenches and rest periods just behind the front, which seemed to be the general pattern for front line troops. There were several arrivals of reinforcements to replace those who had been lost, including both officers and men. During one of these periods on the front, Lieutenant Colonel Vernon was wounded while checking on a saphead held by the boxer, Gerry Delaney. Major H. Pirie took command until Vernon could recover and return.

The German Army spent most of the war in defensive positions. Apart from the initial invasion of Belgium there had been few large attacks by the enemy, until February when there was an attempt by the

136

EXPLOSION DE SAINT-DENIS, 4 Mars 1916

More ruins caused by artillery fire in the towns around the front.

Germans to win the war before the British could get up to full strength. The German plan was for a great attack on the French at Verdan. The battle was to rage for months, with enormous losses on both sides. There were numerous attacks and counter-attacks, when each side pushed the other back before once again retiring. The British were forced to plan a large assault that would take some of the pressure off the French. Plans were drawn up for the Battle of the Somme.

One of the reasons for interviewing the older men in the battalion became clear a few days later when all the men over forty years of age were sent back to base camp to make way for younger men. It had been decided that life in the trenches was too difficult for them. The older men were left sitting around in camp waiting for someone to find them a job. This was to be the end of John Chessire's front line experiences.

The camp had several YMCA and Church Army huts serving food. John's letters began to take on a lighter note, now that he was away from the trenches. Although he seemed to feel that there was still much that the older men had to offer, and that it was his duty to be at the front, he must have felt some relief at not having to go back onto the front line. In one letter, he mentioned that the *Church Times* commented on the lack of religious feeling in the Army and considered this a bonus, as those men with religious feeling found it harder to cope with trench warfare. No doubt he was thinking of soldiers killing other men.

For the first time, John mentioned the emotions that being on the front had stirred in him. He said those at the front did not indulge in the same notions of patriotism that they did at home. Trench warfare had upset all his preconceived ideas of military life being in any way appealing. He thought that the infantry might just as well be described as rat catchers or gravediggers. Nonetheless, if that was what the country needed then John was willing to do his bit.

March finally saw the beginning of conscription at home. This led to an even greater change in the characters of regiments, as men from all walks of life were sent to any unit that was below strength. Private Worger of the 2nd Sportsmen's Battalion said in a letter to his wife that the battalion was practically being turned into an officer training corps. He himself considered applying for a commission. If the chance of a commission was still open to him, then there must have been different conditions applied to the 2nd Battalion at this time than there had been for the 1st Battalion, as Chessire had lost any chance of a commission. It also seems that in their case the older men were not removed from the 2nd Battalion, as Private Worger was over forty and still at the front. If he did get a commission, however, it would mean that he would henceforth have to live on his pay and his wife's allowance from the War Office would stop.

The war and separation from his wife had a significant effect on Private Worger. He felt that the love he had for his wife before the terrible war would be nothing compared to the love he would have for her when he returned home. It was only being married that helped him to get through it all and he wondered how unmarried men coped. He was not to forget the lessons he had learned in hell. Even having water to wash his hands and face became a luxury that he missed. He had at times washed in snow and cold tea.

Going out of the trenches at night was another thing that he hated. Machine-guns would open up on them and they would quickly get down on the floor while bullets flew over their heads. There had been one fatality and two men wounded in the past week. The sportsman in him came out, as he said that the Germans did not play the game and although he claimed to feel no enmity towards the foe, he said that he would kill them without any feeling.

Over the next few months, John Chessire spent his time working at a number of jobs, such as building a YMCA hut. Some of the older men from the 1st Battalion were about to be dispensed with. One of John's friends, Biggs, was in the hospital and it looked as though he was shortly to be sent home to work on his farm. Removing older men was not a popular decision. John pointed out that Biggs' work in the trenches had been equal to that of ten ordinary men, even if they were younger, and he wondered if anyone realised what talent was being wasted.

John worked out a code to tell his wife how much he loved her. He did this by using the letters that describe the hardness of the lead in a pencil, in hopes it would slip past the censor. He asked her if she minded being addressed in these terms:

HH	happy heart
H	heart
HB	beloved
BB	beautiful beloved
BBB	best beautiful beloved

Meanwhile the 1st Battalion was sent to Souchez. The French had taken the area from the Germans in September 1915. The village of Souchez had been completely destroyed in the process. In March, the French handed the area over to the Commonwealth troops, including the Sportsmen. They were 12km north of Arras. The valley that ran through the area was on the western side of Vimy Ridge.

In April, Private Worger had a close shave. He told his wife how a few minutes after leaving his shelter, a trench mortar round blew it to pieces. He went on to explain to her that he did not fear death, although the incident certainly made him think about it. By 1 May, the battalion was at Villers Au Bois, and on 23 May plans were made for an attack at 1.30 p.m., which was then cancelled. Another was planned for 8.15 p.m. along with the Royal Berkshires but this again was cancelled. Unfortunately, the cancellation message did not reach B Company of the Sportsmen, who advanced and took the enemy trench. They held it for an hour and a half before being recalled. There were seven men killed and a further seventy-eight wounded. Mistakes like this resulting from poor communication were a common feature during the war.

At the end of May, John wrote to someone named Frances, who had evidently not written to him for some time. He told her that if she did

Above: *A stereo view of stretcher-bearers rescuing the wounded. They were much overworked at the time of large attacks.*

Opposite: *John sent his wife this drawing. It reminded him of his old watering can at a spring bank, which presumably was located at one of his old homes. The drawing he copied it from is called* De leau vous plait de suite. *(C. Chaloner)*

not write soon he would have to come home to talk to her, but that she would probably not want to see him unless he came home without an arm, a leg or half a face. Frances must have been one of the many back at home who believed that a man's place was at the front, until he was no longer capable of fighting. John told her that he had given a shirt to a young Scotch boy who had lost half his face. Although John had claimed to be the first member of the battalion to be wounded, his was a small shrapnel wound on the thumb and nothing like the serious wounds that others suffered

By the beginning of June, John had expected to be sent back to England, although he was unsure for what purpose, or where he would go, but within a few days he could tell that he was not going home. Then came news of the sudden death of Lord Kitchener, killed when his ship was sunk by a German U-boat. Although Kitchener's death was a surprise, John did not see it as much of a blow, believing that the death of great men usually preceded victory. It may be that his religion provided him with the means to rationalise such developments, as being part of some altogether greater plan.

John's opinion was not shared by many people at home. Kitchener had earned himself a great reputation and it was this status that led to the ill-fated voyage to Russia. It was hoped that his presence in the country would inspire the Russian population in their struggle against the Germans. Kitchener's death came as a great shock to many. Dorothy Thomas, of Hythe, in Kent, remembered hearing the name Kitchener and the town hall being mentioned when she was young. Thinking Kitchener was at the hall, she went there only to find a large crowd reading the latest war bulletin in the window. She ran home to tell her father the news of Kitchener's death. He was so horrified that he went to read the news himself before he could believe it. Symptomatic of a public mourning the loss of their powerful figurehead were the rumours that began to circulate across Britain that Kitchener was not in fact dead but engaged on a secret mission. He would return once his mission was complete, reminiscent of the legend of King Arthur, who was supposed to come back when England needed him.

The 1st Battalion had by then moved to Carency but the Germans still had control of Vimy Ridge. Much of the fighting in the area took place underground. Tunnels were dug and packed with large mines that left large craters when they exploded, many of which are still visible today. Despite this underground conflict, the battalion still suffered casualties most days when on the front line.

By July, the battle at Verdun between the Germans and French had been underway for five months. A report in *The Times* stated that it was the prowess of the French Army that was saving France. Nonetheless, there were large numbers of wounded men and a French Wounded Emergency Fund was begun to raise money for French hospitals. July saw the duty of the battalion take a serious turn when they learned they were to be posted to the Somme. The average life expectancy on the Somme was just three weeks and many men died within a week of arriving from England. The battalion was to be involved in some of the fiercest fighting of the battle, including the battle of Deville Wood. However, the impending battle did not stop sport at home. At Lords, there was a cricket match between the Irish Guards and Artist Rifles, who had moved into Hare Hall Camp in Romford, the previous home of the 2nd Sportsmen.

The Times published a letter from an anonymous officer to his parents, written the day before the Battle of the Somme began. He stated that he had never felt more confident and cheerful in his life, and would not miss the coming attack for anything. 'Every man and officer is happy and cheerful. It is impossible to fear death when one is no longer an individual but a member of a regiment, and of an Army. To be killed means nothing

SPORTSMAN'S BATTALION. First Innings.

Private E. G. Hayes	b Bristowe	0
Private A. Sandham	l b w, b Bristowe	21
Private E. Hendren	c Skinner, b Longden	35
Private W. E. Bates	c Coverdale, b Bonsor	57
Capt. H. J. Inglis	c Napper, b Bristowe	1
Capt. N. Cockell	c Holland, b Longden	51
Private A. Webb	b Coverdale	93
Private H. Penfold	not out	36
Lieut. W. A. Rutherford		
Private A. Smith		
Sergeant E. L. Marsden		
	B 15, lb 2	17

Total for 7 Wickets 311

Umpires—Private F. L. Evans and Private J. Cheston.

Scorers—Private R. H. Pavitt and Private W. W. Sawden.

HON. ARTILLERY COMPANY v. SPORTSMAN'S BATTALION.
SATURDAY, JUNE 12th, 1915.

HON. ARTILLERY. First Innings.

Private O. C. Bristowe	c Hayes, b Bates	53
Private W. A. Batchelor	b Penfold	4
Private H. Coverdale	b Hayes	20
Private H. E. S. Skinner	b Hayes	1
C.-Q.-M.-S. R. Hargreaves	b Hayes	37
Private H. B. Kidd	c Smith, b Bates	3
Private A. S. Holland	b Hayes	0
Corpl. D. D. Napper	b Penfold	7
Private W. G. Longden	b Marsden	36
Private H. J. Bonsor	l b w b Bates	12
Private N. W. Beeson	not out	2
	B 15, l-b 3	18

Total 193

This page and opposite: *The Sportsmen's cricket team played at Lords in June 1915, one year before the devastation of the Somme, and soundly defeated the Hon Artillery Co. Both teams included well-known cricketers of the period.*

but it is only you who suffer. You really pay the cost.' The officer was supposedly killed the next day, on the infamous and bloody first day of the Somme.

There were inevitable casualties amongst the 2nd Battalion of the Sportsmen. Private W. Stephenson wrote to his wife on 1 July, telling her that he might soon get leave but that only two men per battalion were given leave at a time. Stephenson was a professional golfer and club maker before enlisting. He started his letter with the line that he was still alive and kicking and went on to mention that the 2nd Sportsmen were the hardest worked battalion in France and that this had even been brought up in parliament. Private Stephenson stated that he could see nothing but barbed wire in front of him, and the 'shelling made him get the wind up-bang!' He asked his wife how his fourth child was, a daughter, Yvonne, born in 1916. Stephenson never finished his letter. Called away to go on a raid, he died later that day and never got to see his new daughter.

There seemed to be little that was secret about the coming battle. Even German newspapers were asking when the British offensive was coming. The Somme attack was scheduled to take place after an eight-day artillery bombardment of the German lines. This involved 1,500 guns, which were supposed to have destroyed any enemy opposition by the time the British troops attacked and two large mines were exploded. Nearly three quarters of a million men took part in the attack. Amongst them morale was high. The close-knit nature of the Pals Battalions provided mutual friendship and support. Most of the men believed in the plan and were confident that the advances were going to be easy after the tremendous artillery bombardment.

The area of the Somme had been quiet for most of the war, giving the Germans time to build strong and deep defences. The existence of most of these deep bunkers was unknown to the British. The majority of the men that had assembled to take part in the attack were new units just out from England and included many of the Pals Battalions.

The plan for the attack seemed quite simple. It worked on the principle that one wave of men often failed in an attack. Two waves were sometimes successful, and three waves even more so. Working on this hypothesis, in their wisdom the Army sent four waves, but despite the almost complete destruction of the first wave, and the discovery that the wire was still in place, the other waves were still sent over the top. There was no way to send messages back, as the first waves were trapped between the German front and the enemy artillery barrage behind them.

OFFICIAL PHOTOGRAPH, CROWN COPYRIGHT RESERVED.

BRITISH MINE EXPLODING AT BEAUMONT HAMEL. Nº13

One of the first events of the Battle of the Somme began with the mine at Beaumont Hamel.

The Germans on the front line had taken shelter during the bombardment and their defences, including the deep concrete bunkers, were hardly touched. Many of the British shells were duds. Even the barbed wire protecting the German trenches was not completely destroyed. Once the British barrage stopped, the Germans came out of the bunkers to face the attack and had plenty of time to set up their machine-guns. Many of the advancing men were cut down by machine-gun fire the moment they climbed out of the trenches during the first attack on 1 July. The rest were cut down as they walked slowly across No Man's Land or were taken out by German artillery.

The British artillery finished shelling the German front line and moved on to the areas behind it in preparation for further advances. Consequently, the Germans on the front line, emerging from their bunkers, were untroubled by any hostile artillery. A sergeant in the 3rd Tyneside Irish remembered how he saw his men fall under the onslaught of the machine-guns. The fire was so successful that he felt as though he was the only man left.

There was a very good example of the sporting instincts of the British Army during the battle, although not from the Sportsmen's Battalion on this occasion. There had been precedents in the war of attacking forces kicking footballs in front of them, out across No Man's Land. One such example occurred at Loos in 1915 when the 1st Battalion of the 18th London Regiment attacked. The most famous incident of this occurred when Captain W. Neville of the 8th East Surreys bought four footballs during his leave. As they prepared to attack, he gave one ball to each platoon and offered a prize for the first ball to be kicked into the German trenches. The men kicked the balls out of the trench and followed them. Sadly the prize was never awarded, as Captain Neville died soon after leaving the trench. It was not only footballs that were kicked across No Man's Land: the 8th Battalion of the London Irish Regiment kicked a rugby ball in front of them as they went over the top.

It was manifest from the first day, when 58,000 casualties were suffered by the British, that the artillery bombardment had failed. Nearly 20,000 of these casualties were fatal. Instead of cancelling the attack, Sir Douglas Haig sent more waves over in the following days with similarly bloody results. Any gains which made were often lost again within days, but the battle raged for months. Even the eventual introduction of tanks in September had little effect. The Somme will forever be known as a terrible battle that led to a senseless loss of life.

David Lloyd George believed that the battle destroyed the old German Army, killing its best men and officers. However, it led to the deaths of the best British and French men as well. The battle was mainly fought by the volunteers of 1914–15, who he described as the best of Britain's young manhood. The Battle of the Somme was widely reported in newspapers at home, but it is hard to believe that the stories were covering the battle we now know so much about. On 4 July, *The Times* reported that on the third day of the battle the fiercest fighting was in the centre of the twenty-mile battlefront, near the villages of La Boselle and Orvillers. According to the report, the British made some advances and maintained the ground gained. The German garrison did put up a great fight but over 12,300 enemy prisoners were taken.

Several trainloads of wounded men from the Somme arrived in London. They were reported to be cheerful. One man said that the supply of shells fired by the British artillery was wonderful. Apart from large attacks, there were also smaller raids taking place on the northern part of the front. These were mainly reconnaissance in force but often turned into mini-attacks. According to the newspapers, the attack had been a complete success on the part of the British and French. There had been detailed reports on each position, and the wounded were portrayed as being undaunted and in good humour. The large proportion of the wounded were suffering from minor wounds, which meant that the total number of those afflicted with permanent disabilities was to be small. Despite the supposedly detailed reporting, there was no mention in the press of the thousands who had died. Some reports in the press were so distorted that the men on the front line could not believe that they were connected to what they had experienced. Lord Northcliffe, the owner of *The Times*, wrote that the open-air life the soldiers enjoyed and their lack of responsibility kept them happy and fit.

The British artillery was reported to have been extremely destructive and so thorough that German prisoners said they expected the attack days earlier. There was only the slightest hint that not all was quite as it should have been: 'As always there were places where individual parts of trenches and barbed wire miraculously escaped destruction and this caused considerable losses.' One had to read between the lines of the press reports to get close to the truth.

Reports were printed explaining how after the German positions were captured the British troops found elaborate subterranean barracks and fortified positions. Some dugouts were up to 30ft deep. There were other clues in the newspapers as to how the battle was really going. The list of officers that had died at the front and was published in the newspapers was getting longer each day.

The romantic concept of the great British sportsman was still a common feature in the thoughts of men going into battle and in the collective mind of the nation. A report of an officer's death in *The Times*, on 19 July, was entitled, 'A Cricketers Last Message'. Second Lieutenant Frederick Bertram Key, of the Royal Warwickshire Regiment, had been a member of Lichfield Cricket Club. In a letter that was to be sent to his parents in the event of his death, he said, 'If you receive this you will know that I have been bowled out, middle peg. You can be sure however that I batted well.'

The attitudes of the men involved in the attack are difficult to understand today, but are vividly illustrated in H. Russell's personal account of his experience on the first day of the Somme. He belonged to the Rifle Brigade, and his amazing recollections show the powerful and single-minded mentality of these men doing what had to be done. Russell went over the top on the first day of the Somme. He remembered a thick smokescreen covering the attack, but when they came out of the smoke they were sitting targets for the German machine-gunners. He said that many men fell but that did not worry him, until he realised that there were very few men from the attacking front line still capable of going on. He dove into a shell hole for cover. While trying to decide what to do next, he was joined in the hole by a young officer. The lieutenant said that he had been ordered to go on at any cost. As he stood up to climb out of the hole, he was immediately riddled with bullets and fell back into the hole, dead. Russell then decided that he should perservere, despite the fact that it meant almost certain death. He stood up and was hit twice, falling back into the hole but still alive. The soldiers of the British Army clearly did not share the view of George Patton, who gained fame in the Second World War but who also fought in the First World War, when he said, 'No one ever won a war by dying for their country but only by making some poor bastard die for theirs.'

At first, Russell felt that he was being brave by attempting to go on. He later realised that once he had made the decision he felt no fear, as he knew that he would be dead within the next few seconds. He came to the conclusion that once a man realises that death is certain, he does not fear it anymore. It never seemed to occur to him that his death was to serve no purpose at all. Russell resolved to try and make his way back. He crawled to another shell hole where he met a comrade, who was also wounded. The man said to him that they may end up in the same hospital. Russell felt that he was being overly optimistic. This proved to be the case, as a shell then landed in the hole killing his friend and further wounding Russell. By now he felt that he was so badly wounded that he could not possibly survive and thought about killing himself. Someone had told him that drinking spirits when suffering from serious open wounds was fatal. Having a bottle of rum with him, he made up his mind to drink it. The spirit actually had the reverse effect and made him feel better, and once darkness fell he crawled back to the British trenches, which took him hours.

Soldiers of different nationalities were portrayed in the media as having different strengths. The British considered their troops to be the best at fighting. Others argued that troops from the colonies were the best soldiers. Reports in German newspapers on the Battle of the Somme indicated that the attacks by the French were the hardest for the German troops to deal with.

Despite the terrible cost of the battle, the men did not seem too downhearted. The 10th Essex was involved in the beginning of the battle. They then had a short period of rest but were aware they would

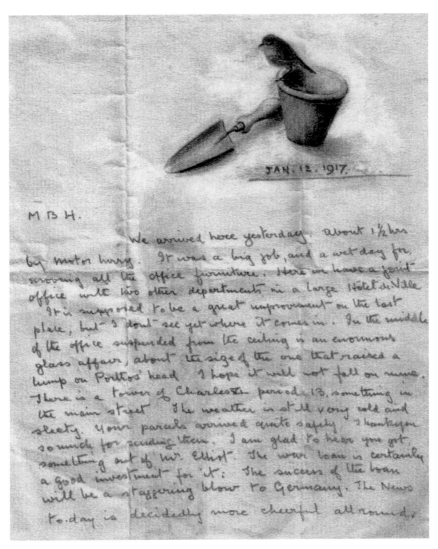

M B H.

We arrived here yesterday, about 1½ hrs
by motor lorry. It was a big job, and a wet day for
moving all the office furniture. Here we have a joint
office with two other departments in a large Hôtel de Ville
It is supposed to be a great improvement on the last
place, but I don't see yet where it comes in. In the middle
of the office suspended from the ceiling is an enormous
glass affair, about the size of the one that raised a
lump on Poilu's head. I hope it will not fall on mine.
There is a tower of Charleston period, 13, something in
the main street. The weather is still very cold and
sleety. Your parcels arrived quite safely. I thank you
so much for sending them. I am glad to hear you got
something out of Mr. Elliot. The war loan is certainly
a good investment for it; the success of the loan
will be a staggering blow to Germany. The News
to-day is decidedly more cheerful all round.

A letter from John Chessire with a small illustration at the top. (C. Chaloner) soon be sent out on another attack. They commented that they did not mind where or when it took place.

The Sportsmen's Battalion played a big part in the battle for Deville Wood although it was the South Africans who got most of the credit for taking the wood. The 2nd South African Regiment had numbered over 3,000 men when they went into the wood on 15 July. They held it for a few days, while the front line was nothing more than connected shell holes. Only just over 700 came out again when they were relieved on 19 and 20 July. On the flank of the South Africans were the 10th Essex and 8th Norfolk Regiment. They were heavily counter-attacked and driven out as other units were sent in. The ferocity of the fighting is shown by the fact that only just over 100 of the South African dead have known graves. A letter written by one of the South African soldiers said that no quarter was given by either side. When they first entered the wood, the foliage was so thick that they could not see more than ten yards. Within days the area was reduced to bare tree stumps.

The part played by the South Africans was extensively reported in the newspapers. It was recorded on 18 July that the South Africans attacked Deville Wood with great gallantry. They went right through the wood and displayed resourcefulness and skill in overcoming the difficulties involved in this type of fighting. Casualties were reported to be none too heavy. On 19 July, the press claimed that Deville Wood had been counter-attacked by the Germans and that there was heavy fighting still in progress. The attack was preceded with gas and lachrymatory shells. Part of the wood was recaptured by the Germans but only with heavy losses on their part.

Reports on 20 July were contradictory. One paragraph in *The Times* noted that the part of Deville Wood that the Germans had recaptured had again been taken by the South Africans. The next paragraph said that a German counter-attack had driven overseas [South African] troops down to the southern part of the wood. There they were reinforced, and despite another German attack, held on to the area they had taken.

The wood was shelled so heavily that it was described as being like a great subterranean fire, which sent jets and spits of flames bursting from thousands of fissures in the ground.

On 25 July, there was a report on the South Africans' part in the battle for the wood, supported by a Scottish regiment. The South Africans had taken the wood on 15 July but then suffered heavy losses under artillery fire. The trenches were destroyed and small bands of the South Africans came out of the wood before stopping at the Scottish lines, where they remained to help prevent the Germans from coming any further.

On 27 July, *The Times* printed a report on the splendid bravery of the South Africans. There was a special order by the brigadier general of the South African Brigade in France. He expressed his high regard and admiration of the gallantry and dogged determination in capturing and holding for three days and nights Deville Wood. There is no doubt that the South Africans did a great job in taking the wood and in holding part of it against several counter-attacks. What is surprising is that their courage was praised so highly in the press while the efforts of others who also took part in the battle were mainly ignored.

John Chessire was back in a camp far behind the lines. His letters from this time do not mention the battle of Deville Wood nor any of the other members of the battalion, with whom he seems to have lost contact.

In the days before their part in the battle for Deville Wood, the battalion was in the trenches near Bernefay Wood where they were heavily shelled on 27 July, suffering numerous casualties. Some of the shells contained gas, but a breeze blew most of it away before the battalion moved forward. Headquarters was in a dugout, which turned out to be the last shelter dug by the famous sculler, Albany, who was killed shortly after completing it. During the move up to the trenches at the edge of Deville Wood there were some distressing conditions in store for the Sportsmen. The dead had not been buried because of the fierce fighting and recent hot weather had left a terrible atmosphere. The South Africans who had occupied the position previously had again been beaten back. The Sportsmen were to attack, along with the King's Royal Rifle Battalion and the Royal Berkshires.

The following morning the battalion experienced its first attack, including all four companies, with an artillery barrage preceding them. Unfortunately, one shell fell short and wounded one of the members of the battalion. The wounded man was supposedly very aggrieved, not at the artillery, but at the lost opportunity of at last getting to grips with the enemy. They took up position in a trench at the edge of the woods, ready to attack the following morning. Despite it being their first time over the top, the men were reported to be in good spirits. One man was pleased that he had time to finish his breakfast before they went over. The woods were full of German machine-guns, so it had to have been retaken by that time. Artillery fire also landed on the edge of the wood. In the ensuing skirmish Captain Grant was killed, along with another twenty-six men from other ranks. Twenty men were unaccounted for and 143 wounded.

Despite these losses, the Sportsmen took as their target the trench in the middle of the wood. They held the position against a number of counter-attacks and an artillery barrage that lasted all day. The barrage completely destroyed the woods, turning it into a landscape of tree stumps. Captain Walsh collected all the carrying parties, which numbered 250 men, and formed them into a fighting force. A number of prisoners were taken, some of whom sheltered in a shell hole and had to be forced to move back by Sergeant Major Powney, who was killed later that day. One of the hardest objectives was a redoubt with machine-guns that caused numerous casualties. None of the wounded could be evacuated because of heavy fire. It was during this battle that the boxer Jerry Delaney died.

There were so many officers wounded and killed that during an officer's conference with the brigadier in a shell hole, Corporal Walker came to take part because he was in command of the machine-gun company. The history of the Royal Fusiliers reveals that the wood was overrun again on 27 July, and that the place of honour in the fighting went to the 1st Sportsmen. By 29 July, the strength of the battalion was reduced to eighteen officers and 400 other ranks. The battalion was relieved at dawn and went back to Bernefay. There had been nearly 400 casualties, 60 per cent of the men who had begun the attack. Out of eighteen officers, thirteen were casualties. One high point was that the men found a large number of German cigars and were smoking them as they withdrew.

There was a strange lack of publicity as to the Sportsmen's part in the battle for Deville Wood, especially after the furore given to the South African part in its capture. The report in *The Times* on 29 July stated that the British were holding the lower part of the wood, while the Germans held the upper part. Following a rolling barrage, there was an attack that cleared the wood. This must have been a report of the attack by the Sportsmen but they were never mentioned, and nor was any other unit that took part.

On 31 July, *The Times* reported that stern fighting was taking place in the wood, stating solemnly that nothing could compare with the artillery barrage upon the wood. There had been four separate attacks since 27 July, all of which had been beaten back with determination and severe losses. This must have been the Sportsmen but again they were not mentioned.

A battalion commander supposedly reported how he went to speak to a soldier who had fallen over with exhaustion after two days' fighting without a break in the wood. There was no point trying to wake him, so he was left to sleep. Conditions in the wood were so hard that an attack was often undertaken at a crawl and involved scrambling in and out of shell holes. However, nothing could exceed the pluck displayed by those whose job it was to treat the wounded.

There was a comment on the publicity relating to the battle when the Sportsman came out of the wood. One of the officers was making out a casualty return in a shell hole by the light of burning trees. The quartermaster handed him a newspaper and told him that he would find something interesting in it. This turned out to be a full column describing how the South Africans had taken the wood.

On 30 July, the 2nd Battalion of the Sportsmen moved onto the front line at Deville Wood. They then took part in a successful advance on a German trench on the far side of the wood. One of the 2nd Battalion's casualties was Private Worger. He had been writing a letter to his wife, saying how he was feeling fit and well. Before he finished the letter, he was called away to go on duty and was killed when carrying the wounded out of Deville Wood on a stretcher. Amongst his papers, now in the Imperial War Museum, is a counterfoil from a 5s postal order with a message written on the back: 'Whoever finds this please send to this address'. It was his wife's address and the counterfoil was in his pay book. Worger's papers include several letters from other men in his company to his wife. One of these was from Hylton Cleaver, who told Worger's wife that he had been a close friend of her husband, and that he had also been wounded. He went on to detail for her the circumstances of her husband's death, taking place under heavy fire and while carrying a stretcher with a wounded man. He had previously been told to rest but had only done so for twenty minutes. It seems that, despite the difficulties Worger had with training, he had overcome them to become a very effective soldier, despite being over forty years of age.

Another letter came to Worger's wife from a Private Cassidy, who had found his pay book with the postal order counterfoil on his body. He described how her husband had been buried as respectfully as shelling would allow. Worger's wife wrote back to Cassidy asking if there had been a service at her husband's grave. Cassidy clearly had difficulty wording his reply. He explained that the burial had been carried out under heavy shelling and so there had been no time for a service, as the burial party were under threat all the time. There was yet another letter from a man in the Mill Road hospital, who told Mrs Worger that he had been shocked to hear of her husband's death. It seems that just before this happened, he had been saved by Private Worger after lying wounded for some time. He described her husband as a cheerful and reassuring character, relaying for her how Worger had told him that he had 'coped a blighty one', before carrying him back to safety.

In early August, the battalion went back to Deville Wood, relieving the 1st Liverpool. Lieutenant Colonel R. Barnett Barker was in command of the wood. The battalion had increased its numbers slightly, with twenty-one officers and 449 other ranks. Some of this increase in numbers was due to men who had eventually turned up after they withdrew from the woods following the initial attack. During this second spell in the woods, Lieutenant Holmes was wounded. Seven men were killed and another sixteen wounded due to the almost continuous shelling. They were relieved again on 3 August. Two days later Captain Miller, of the Royal Army Medical Corps, went into the wood with stretcher-bearers to retrieve the body of Captain A. McDougall. Also during August, one of the tanks used by the British managed to get round the back of Deville Wood. Many of the Germans manning the trenches in front of the wood fled but the tank was destroyed and the attack failed.

Around this time John Chessire mentioned good news from the Somme in his letters but did not expand on it. On 27 August, he disclosed further pleasing news, explaining that they had at last got hold of Thiepval. By the end of the month, he alluded to the Worcesters and Warwick's having distinguished themselves.

By the beginning of September, the 1st Battalion was back on the front line. They had been expecting a rest after the battle but after travelling through several districts they found themselves returning to the trenches. They later moved to Hebuterne to relieve the Coldstream Guards. Hebuterne was a village south of Gommecourt which had been fought over by the French during the 2nd battle of Artois in June 1915. The village was close to the allied lines and often shelled. The civilians moved out during the battle and the village was fortified, and so the military inhabitants had a level of luxury not available in other places. The dugouts were furnished with the contents of the houses in the village; it was not unusual to find four-poster beds in dugouts.

Tanks were thought to be weapons that were going to change the outcome of the war. Unfortunately, they were so mechanically unreliable that they had little effect.

There were adaptations to the front line in the area, where gas experts fitted pipes along the parapet. These pipes pumped gas into No Man's Land, but some of this would then drift back onto the troops in the trench. By the beginning of September the Canadians had been taken over the stores. John found dealings with them difficult when getting his officers' rations.

On 12 September, Lieutenant Fisher, of the 1st Battalion, took out a patrol into No Man's Land and was killed by machine-gun fire. On 15 September another patrol, led by Second Lieutenant Martin, with twenty-five other ranks, planned to raid the German trenches. The objective, as described in the battalion diary, was to secure identification and harass the Germans. Raiding parties were often armed with unusual weapons. The men would take knives and cudgels, so fighting was expected to take place at very close quarters. No doubt, this would help to remove the loss of instinct to fight after long periods of inaction.

There was a pre-raid plan, which was similar to a full attack. On the evening of 16 September, there was to be an 8.30 gas discharge on the enemy trench. At 10.00 p.m., an artillery bombardment was to ensue for ten minutes, followed by half a minute of fire from a Stokes mortar. At 10.45 p.m., intense artillery bombardment was to start, followed by Stokes mortar fire for one minute. Meanwhile, machine-gun fire was to be used to stop the Germans repairing wire, between 8.00 and 10.40 p.m. The raid was to be in three sections. The right section had four bombers and two bayonet men. The centre section was to have two bombers and ten bayonet men, while the left matched the right section. The bayonet men were to have thirty-five rounds and two bombs. Each man was to take his gas helmet, and 50 per cent of the men would carry wire cutters. There was to be no more than ten minutes spent in the enemy trench and withdrawal would be signalled by a klaxon. The password to get safely back into the British trench was 'Bees'.

Although the planning for the raid was written up in detail, the results of the event were patchier. Lieutenant Martin shot one German in the face and missed another, but that was the only definite detail of the conflict in the diary. Eleven Germans were supposedly killed, but it was believed that the real number was closer to twenty. Ten prisoners were brought back. There were no casualties amongst the raiding party, and every raider had blood on his club or bayonet. None of the accounts depict how it must have been for the men involved in such close-up killing. Fighting the enemy with a club or knife must be very different than shooting them from a distance.

There was a very unusual event on 6 October, when a member of the 1st Battalion was court-martialled, the only example I could find of this happening to a member of the battalion. Private Allingham was charged with drunkenness on active service and was sentenced to three months of hard labour. This sentence was then commuted to ninety days' field punishment by Brigadier General Kellet.

In October, the 1st Battalion was moved to Redan Ridge. This was the previous site of a battle which took place in July, when a large mine had been detonated in the area. On 20 October, a dugout was damaged by shellfire and eight men were buried alive. They managed to dig out six of them but the other two were covered with so much earth that the decision was made to leave them there. Of the six who were pulled out, two were wounded and two suffering from shell shock. There was little news of the war in John's October letters, although he did bring up an article by Stanley Baldwin on 'Trade Disputes'. He made an interesting comment about how the result of such disputes would depend on how the forces were treated when they returned to the Promised Land.

The 1st Battalion took part in the Battle of Beaumont Hamel, in November, the last large battle of the year. This time it was a success and Beaumont Hamel was captured. The men that took part in this battle, including the Sportsmen, were far more battle-hardened than those fresh recruits who had taken part in the opening exchanges of the Battle of the Somme in July. The original assault on Beaumont Hamel had been back in July. A tunnel had been dug to the sunken road, so that the attack would begin closer to the German trenches. The action had been preceded by the explosion of a large mine, which was filmed by Geoffrey Malins, the official war filmmaker. Unfortunately, the attack failed, mainly due to the power of the German machine-guns. There was also the matter of the underground bunkers, which had protected the Germans from artillery barrage and from which they had emerged to drive back the attackers. A correspondent from *The Times* watched the attack on Beaumont Hamel in July and noted how the village had disappeared after a forty-eight-hour artillery barrage. In September, the war poet Edward Blunden was in the area while serving with the 11th Royal Sussex Regiment. He related how the area was nothing but ruins, including the village church which had a large bell amongst the rubble, used by the Army as a gas warning alarm.

Now after being the site of one of the first battles of the Somme, Beaumont Hamel was also one of the last. The attack began on 13 November, led by the 5th Army. The Royal Naval Division took the German lines and reached Beaumont Hamel. To their left, the 51st Highland Division followed them. The 16th Light Highland Infantry got as far as Frankfurt Trench but were then cut off and finally had to surrender. Frankfurt Trench later became the site of a military cemetery.

The Sportsmen's Battalion were sent in to reinforce the Highland Light Infantry on the Green Line on 13 November. This was in the southern part of the line close to Redan Ridge. Companies B and D took the German second line. On 14 November, the battalion moved forward in support of the Kings Royal Rifle Corps and Royal Berks. Companies A and C reached Crater Lane and then Wagon Road. Companies B and D reached Lager Alley. The Sportsmen also took part in an unsuccessful attack on Munich Trench with the 2nd Highland Light Infantry, which was close to the village of Serre. On 16 November, they moved back, and 18 November marked the end of the Battle of the Somme.

The reports of the battle in newspapers at home described the capture of Beaumont Hamel by 15 November but also stated that the picture was far from clear, as the battlefield was wrapped in thick fog. Reports went on to describe how the Germans had believed Beaumont Hamel to be invincible. The ridge on which the village stood was a honeycomb of dugouts and underground defences. There was also a system of ancient caves, all of which had been used so effectively in July.

This time the defences did not work, as the allied attackers found the first few lines poorly defended and quickly overran them. Any Germans who did come up from underground found themselves cut off by attackers who had already taken the area behind them. It was reported that one battalion of an English county regiment had taken over 300 prisoners.

In a strange coincidence, a member of the 2nd Sportsmen's Battalion, Private Arthur Dorman, was killed on 13 November. His brother, Lieutenant Temporary Captain Anthony Dorman MC, of the 13th Service Battalion East York's Regiment, was killed on the same day. They are both commemorated in St Mary's Church, in Warbleton, East Sussex.

The 2nd Battalion of the Sportsmen played a part in the battle of Beaumont Hamel and was stationed in Buster trench. Private Edward Minty Miller enlisted in the 2nd Battalion in February 1915. Although born in Ceylon, Miller, had been educated at St Faiths, in Cambridge and Marlborough. He was the son of Archdeacon Miller of Ceylon, who later became vicar of Pampisford, Cambridge. Private Miller was killed at Beaumont Hamel on 13 November 1916 at the age of thirty-four. His captain wrote that he was a good soldier and willing worker, a man he was sorry to lose, and for whom he had great hopes. He was always ready to undertake any job to help other men and always willing to do more than his share of the work.

Another famous fusilier died during the Battle of Beaumont Hamel but was not a member of either of the Sportsmen's battalions. H.H. Munro, the writer better known as Saki, was killed by a sniper. He was a member of the 22nd Service Battalion Royal Fusiliers. His presence there at all was strange, considering the order for the removal of older men from frontline work: he was forty-five when he was killed.

By 18 November, the British forces had gained 12km of ground on the Somme when bad weather brought an end to the battle. The cost of the ground won had been over 400,000 British and 200,000 French casualties. Many of the men involved came from the Pals Battalions. The Germans had fallen back but as a result were in better defended positions.

John Chessire observed a kind of ceremony taking place in the cemetery where he was stationed, something to do with two years of war. He describes the cemeteries close to the lines as beautifully kept. Each grave had a wooden cross with the name and regiment of the deceased on it. He said that unfortunately the cemeteries were often messed up by shellfire but were soon put right again. He commented to his wife that the men had to take the *Daily Mail* in France. He was not a fan of the 'Khaki Articles' they published. He thought that the soldier's language was impossible to reproduce in a newspaper. 'If you take the swear words out there is nothing left.'

John predicted a hard winter in the trenches, as most work was done at night and winter nights were much longer than summer ones. It would mean a much greater expense in starlight flares – when they fell on the barbed wire it gave the impression that the posts were moving. The Germans also had parachute lights that hung in the sky, whose lights were more effective than the British ones. John Chessire wrote that the Germans were complaining that the British had the best artillery, the best airmen and the most shells. He doubted that the Germans would hold out much longer. 'They cannot afford to lose 250,000 men a month like they did in August,' he said. He also remarked on the battalion, wistfully saying that there was probably no one left that he knew, especially since the Big Push. He mentioned the names of some men who died and some who were badly wounded.

Things were hard at home for John's wife. Dorothy's allowance had ended with the death of her father, making them £100 a year worse off. In one letter, he commented that all officers were in debt. He intended to get a job and concluded that it was a good thing that he did not get a commission, for if he had then Dorothy would not be able to manage without the separation allowance.

John saw German prisoners being brought in, dazed like lunatics. He pointed out another of his inventions – a shield made from wire netting, covered in muslin and dipped in mud. The men would be able to use these by crawling to the German trenches and hiding under them until they could be thrown up, when the men would charge out. John told his wife that without public schools the men who controlled the colonies would not have been able to cope. The British colonies would end up like those run by other countries, who did not have gentlemen.

There was still a policy of removing older men from the line, but John mentioned in another letter how some new arrivals at his base were very

A FORECAST OF THE FINISH. BY REGINALD CLEAVER

A rather optimistic view of the final results of the Big Push from the press of the time.

old soldiers. One of them had over twenty years of service in the forces. After the Battle of the Somme, the battalion found itself once again in the pattern of days on the front line, followed by short breaks in the rear in a number of different sectors. John made an interesting observation of the British Tommy in one of his letters in November: 'They grumble about their food and not being used to good food do not realise how well off they are. They always think that someone else is doing better than them.' John seemed to have given up entirely on the idea of a commission. He said that a junior officer requires even more youth than a private and should not be over twenty-five. He himself was approaching forty-five. John was told that there were openings in the R.E.C. (Reinforcements Entertainment Committee), who staged plays and comic operas.

In his next letter, John explained he was to be transferred to somewhere on the Somme. The colonel told him that there was no reason for him to leave if he did not want to. He answered that he could not very well refuse. He was not, however, looking forward to the journey or getting used to strangers again.

In early December, John moved to GHQ X111 Corps. It took him twenty-four hours to get there and was a very uncomfortable journey. He was given the job of mapping, working 9.00 a.m. until 11.00 p.m. These were long hours but there was nothing else to do in the place. He was also back within the sound of the guns.

John enjoyed listening to the men discussing the war. He believed that very few of those fighting had any idea what the war was about. This is not really a surprise, as the reasons were very complicated. The men all agreed, however, that no one could understand what trench warfare was like unless they had experienced it.

During December the 1st Battalion was resting, ready to start the New Year with more action. Temporary Major B. Winter of the battalion was supposed to be the fifth member of a court-martial board on Boxing Day at Le Champ Neuf. It turned out that he had not held his commission for long enough, so he was replaced. That may have been an advantage, as the case he would have heard caused some dispute.

Sub Lieutenant Dyet RN was serving in the 63rd Royal Navy Division when he was nominated to stay behind during an attack on 13 November, which must have been the one on Beaumont Hamel. He was later ordered forward but became lost and refused to take an order from a junior officer to move to the front. Instead, he returned to headquarters. Dyet was sentenced to death and shot.

CHAPTER 10

1917

The beginning of 1917 saw the battalion resume the pattern of short periods of front line work and brief rest periods. The 1st Battalion moved to Courcelette early in January. The Courcellette area had been part of the Somme Offensive. Sir Douglas Haig had used the attack in the area to try out the new weapon of the time, the tank. Forty-nine tanks and twelve divisions had taken part in the attack of the previous September; the tanks had not proven successful, as so many broke down. The attack had led to gains of 2km of enemy territory but it was impossible to hold what they had gained.

John Chessire was on the move, as his mapping office moved to a hotel which the unit shared with two other departments. John believed at this time that the war would be over within the next two months.

In the beginning of February, the battalion moved again to Miramount, where an attack was planned for early in the month. Four days before the attack an operational order, 'Number 111', gave three objectives for the attack. The first was called the 'blue line', which was the front line German trench; the second was the 'green line', a support trench; and third was the 'yellow line', which was the rear area. When these lines were drawn on the map they were placed beyond the actual position of the trenches, as the attackers would also have to hold the open ground in front of the trench. The 99th Brigade was to lead the attack on a 500-yard-long front, between West Miramount Road and East Miramount Road. On the right, one and a half companies of the Sportsmen's Battalion were to attack and hold Grandcourt Trench, the 'blue line'. Another one and a half companies would follow, overtake

LENS après la Guerre — Le Théâtre - Theatre

No buildings were immune from attack. These are the ruins of what was once a theatre.

the first wave and take the 'green line', which was over the crest of 'Hill 130'. The 'yellow line' was to be taken by two companies of the 22nd Fusiliers, who would attack in four waves. The second wave of the 22nd was to deal with any enemy left behind. There had been previous cases where dugouts were ignored during an attack. The enemy had left their dugouts and thwarted the attacking force. The last company of the Sportsmen were to join with a company of the 22nd as a flank guard further along the road.

The Sportsmen moved up to the line on 16 February and had a hard time getting through the mud, slush and congestion. When they finally arrived at the front, they were subjected to heavy artillery bombardment. When they eventually attacked, they were raked by heavy machine-gun fire, guns which the British artillery barrage had not touched. The attacking forces became muddled. The attack failed on the right where the 2nd South Staffs were moving forward, which meant that the Germans in that part of the trench could then turn their machine-guns on the Sportsmen. The battle plan was that the attacking force would spend thirty minutes in the 'blue' trench and then move on. Although the attack was failing, the Germans later reported that one group of British soldiers did reach the third objective but no one knows who this was.

Private C. Clark was a member of the Sportsmen's Battalion and took part in the attack to take the trenches near Miramount. His written account is in the Imperial War Museum. He said that there were to be seven waves, the first three intending to take the first trench and the other waves the second. Clark asked the stretcher-bearers before the attack if they could get the major on a stretcher if he was wounded. Their reply was, 'Have a heart he is six and a half feet tall'. Clark also mentioned that his sister had sent him some type of bullet-proof vest, made of metal. This type of body armour was quite common, on sale in colonial stores frequented by the troops. The shields were often sent to men at the front by their relatives. A letter sent to *The Times* in July 1917 concerning body armour requested that the Government provide it for all troops. It would have been interesting to see what results the body armour would have had on casualty rates. There are similar examples of body armour being worn by the enemy.

The British artillery barrage had begun on the day before the attack on 16 February. It had successfully destroyed the wire in front of the first German trench, so the attacking force crossed it without any trouble. Clark remembered men gasping as they fell while crossing No Man's Land. He also heard German soldiers cry for clemency as the Sportsmen reached the enemy trench, which he said was given. Between the trenches was a ridge, which was covered by heavy machine-gun fire. This took a heavy toll on the men. This must have been the hill mentioned between the objectives. Clark described the advance as 'grim gallantry'. The men struggled on as bombs were thrown by both sides. The other attackers from the King's Royal Rifle Corps, who were positioned on the left, were wearing leather jerkins but the Sportsmen were at a disadvantage because their overcoats were caked with heavy mud. Clark was hit and fell onto his back, believing himself to be badly wounded. He wrote that it felt as though his lungs were alight. He did not go back, but two riflemen close to him tried to return and were shot down by machine-gun fire. Clark's left arm was of no use but he was able to throw his water bottle to another badly wounded soldier.

Clark managed to get himself into a shell hole where he found other men, one dying horribly from a lung wound. Another was lifting up his arm with cries of agony. There were two slightly wounded men who attempted to crawl back to safety. Clark said that it would have been better if they had stayed. It seems that, despite being wounded, Clark did

A small girl in a boat, perhaps one of John's daughters. (C. Chaloner)

not consider deserting his duty as others were doing. However, he did not clarify whether they were members of the Sportsmen's Battalion. It was fortunate that Clark remained in his shell hole, as the two men who tried to return were both hit and killed. There were thoughts of fair play on the Sportsman's mind while he lay there wounded. He defended the decision by the Germans machine-gunners to fire on the men, the bad light would have made it difficult for the Germans to realise that the men were already wounded. Clark's wound was bandaged by a member of the rifles who promised to return for him. Eventually, Clark decided to go back and managed to reach a communication trench where he found a first-aid post. The trench was full of badly wounded men who were lying on the ground. When Clark was sent back on his own, he heard that his company commander had been mortally wounded.

The report of the attack in the newspapers at home gave a more positive slant than reports from the men who took part in it. On 19 February, *The Times* reported about the attack on enemy positions opposite Miramont and Petit Miramont. This supposedly took place on a mile and a half front and captured the enemy lines after progressing 1,000 yards into enemy territory. There was also a copy of the German report on the engagement saying that the attack failed – which was closer to what the men who participated said about it. The newspaper report went on to describe how men of the southern counties and Londoners involved in this attack had given a firm lead to the coming year's campaigns. Then there was a hint that perhaps the attack had not been so successful. These clues were often included in press reports, despite the jingoistic headlines. *The Times* printed that the men soon found the task more difficult than expected, due to fog and a thaw that turned the previously frozen hard ground to deep mud. However, they still did more than could have been hoped for by taking 600 German prisoners.

Miramont was protected by a large steep hill but, despite this, the attackers supposedly went beyond their first objective and gained the summit. According to the report, if it were not for the bad weather they would have still been there. There was no mention of the machine-gun fire that swept away the men who did reach the summit. There seems to have been one high point during the advance, when a sergeant managed to get beyond the hill to see what the Germans were up to before he was captured. While being led back to Petit Miramont, a British artillery barrage began which scared his German captors enough to allow the sergeant to escape.

There were rumours circulating at the time that the Germans knew of the planned attack, as the British trenches that were full of men ready to go over the top were shelled heavily just before they began the advance. One rumour was that a deserter had told the Germans what was planned. General Gough also wondered if a deserter was responsible for giving away the battle plan. Desertion on the night before a battle was not uncommon. It could have been that someone carrying rations up to the front became lost and was captured, or something much more sinister.

On 18 February, a court of enquiry investigated statements from German prisoners. German records show that a British prisoner did give away the plans for an attack. It seems to have been a common event for either side to learn of an impending attack from prisoners. Often prisoners would quickly tell their captors about a planned attack before the artillery bombardment began so they would be taken away to the rear away from danger. Some Canadians had a notice pasted

"Daily Mail" WAR PICTURES

OFFICIAL PHOTOGRAPH.
CROWN COPYRIGHT RESERVED.

WOUNDED "TOMMY" TO THE PHOTOGRAPHER: "I'M NOT A GERMAN!"

Above: *A wounded soldier, carried by German prisoners, tells the men around him that he is not a German.*

Opposite: *It was common for men to send home small flowers in their letters. It seemed to represent a sense of survival, growing amongst the ruins. These were preserved in one of John's letters – the stains they made on the paper are quite clear.* (C. Chaloner)

into their pay book with instructions of what to do if captured. In large words it said, 'Keep your mouth shut'. It may have been that someone could no longer stand the war and deserted to the enemy. Although there had been difficulties with men who could not bear the horrors of war from the beginning, it was only in 1917 that shell shock was put forward as a theory. The diagnosis was from the discovery of a medical officer named Charles Myers, but it was thought then that shell shock was caused by damage to the nervous system, usually by heavy bombardment. There are no records of the results found by the court of inquiry. This could mean that results were lost or that they were deliberately withheld. If there was a deserter just before the battle, then he must have come from the Sportsmen or from the Kings Royal Rifle Corps who were both at the front just before the attack commenced. Of course, the positive reports in the newspapers gave no indication of a suspected traitor.

The battalion also had to put up with severe weather conditions, as well as the fighting. It was so cold that drinking water had been delivered to

the front as blocks of ice. Unfortunately, just before the attack a rapid thaw had set in and No Man's Land turned from a firm surface to a sea of soft mud. The attack led to over 200 casualties.

The following month, the battalion moved back to Courcellette and took part in another attack on Grevillers Trench and Lady Leg Ravine. The order for the attack in the battalion diary states that the 99th Brigade would capture Greyvillers Trench in conjunction with attacks by the 18th Division on the left. The date and zero hour was to be decided later. D Company, under Lieutenant Hilder, was to move on the left of the Kings Royal Rifle Corps and capture a ravine. The ravine was reported to have steep sides and a width of 60ft. Bombers would be able to reach all points of the ravine from either side. The ravine was known to have several machine-gun posts and dugouts. The orders stated that it might be necessary for the section to take cover behind the bank of the ravine while dealing with the enemy in it. There were to be four waves, fifty yards apart, with one platoon in each wave. Each wave was to have riflemen and rifle grenadiers, while the first wave would also have a Lewis Gun. The Lewis gunner would find the best place to site the gun and rake the ravine. There was to be a rolling barrage from the British guns to keep the Boche in their dugouts until the men reached their goal. In the event the attack was a success. There were several prisoners taken, and the objective was achieved. Unfortunately, once again, the battalion suffered several casualties.

John Chessire was working on maps at this time and described to his wife how they were reproduced. Initially, they were cut on wax, and were then then rolled in a frame through silk gauze, a kind of silkscreen printing process. By the end of March, John was on the move again but this time the trip was to take only seven hours. John wrote to his wife that now that China and America were also against the Germans, there could be no possibility of the war going on much longer. He revealed his lack of faith in the education of the working class again by saying he believed the Russian Revolution would stir up unrest amongst the Socialists in Britain. Being uneducated, he said, they would not know their history: Britain had already been through a revolution 200 years ago, so did not need another one. Russia was two centuries behind Britain and France 100 years since their revolution, he said.

In April, the battalion moved to Vimy Ridge. The weather turned for the worse again and they arrived at the front during a snowstorm. There was an attack on the ridge by Canadian troops, who took an enemy trench within a half an hour. They later made more gains, including the Schwaben Tunnel. The British 5th Army also attacked further south. The attack was reported in the *Great War* magazine and noted how the Canadians were waiting to attack on 9 April while up to their waists in freezing mud. They went over the top at the pace of a dead march so that they would not get too close to the rolling barrage in front of them. There were four waves of men, each with a separate objective. The furthest wave was two and a half miles from the British front. Despite heavy machine-gun fire from the Germans, the Canadians passed the first objective without even knowing it because the trench had been so badly damaged by the British artillery fire that it was unrecognisable. The second trench was in slightly better condition. The further they went the more vicious the combat became as the Germans began to put up a fight. The Canadians developed a platoon system in which groups of thirty to forty men were under the command of a subaltern, and each group dealt with enemy machine-guns in their own way. Within forty minutes of the attack, the Canadians took the whole of the German front line system.

The aftermath of the attack on Vimy Ridge from an old stereo view.

The Germans in Petit Vimy were so surprised when the Canadians arrived that most of them surrendered without putting up a fight.

The battalion was ordered to advance beyond the captured ridge, and on 13 April they captured Bailleul Village. John described the capture of Vimy Ridge as the best news of the war. One platoon of Sportsmen mistakenly advanced on Oppy, which was still strongly held, and captured several men, along with some artillery pieces.

John put in his letter that his wife should have heard how well the men were doing and how the Hun could not be very happy in their position. Easter brought a gift for the men who John was stationed with – new gas helmets with ammonia tanks and rubber tubes. The old ones were out of date. John talked about Cyril, his brother who was also serving in the area. He believed that he was with a Northampton Labour Company, which he thought were a rough lot. He wondered why Cyril did not apply to be a draughtsman in a Royal Engineers office.

Not all members of the 1st Battalion spent their time in victorious advances. A Mr Brooks was taken prisoner. His diary gives some details of how prisoners of the Germans were treated. At times they ate nettles and dandelions, as they were not given food by their captors. There were times when Brooks ate mouldy bread off the floor. Despite the men being engaged in heavy manual work, there was very little food to go round. The German guards often directed violence towards prisoners. One form of punishment saw men tied against trees. There seems to be less evidence of similar treatment of German prisoners by the British.

There was still no sign of John becoming disillusioned with the war. His only criticism was that he thought Britain should have been better prepared and gone to war against Germany much earlier.

There was a new commander for the 1st Sportsmen's Battalion. Major E.A. Winter took over after Lieutenant Colonel Vernon went on leave. John mentioned Winter being present at the place where he was working and told his wife that he was by then a major with a Military Medal. John remembered how good Winter had been to their children when they visited John at Tidworth. Winter was later promoted to lieutenant colonel after Vernon became a brigadier general.

In May, the 1st Battalion was in the reserve trench before they took over the whole divisional front. The remnants of the battalion formed two companies, with two companies of the 1st Royal Berks. There were around 100 men in each company. They took part in another attack on Oppy on the night of 2 May. The task given to the battalion during the attack was to capture part of Fresnoy Trench. Although they were successful, there was a slight loss of direction, which meant that the enemy was still occupying the trench to the north. This seemed to happen often during attacks. While clearing the rest of the trench, about seventy German prisoners were taken. The battalion was then successful in meeting up with the Canadians, who had attacked at the south end of the trench.

There was a heavy counter-attack the next day, which pushed them back before they launched a counter-attack themselves and once more took the trench. Following this success they were forced back by a lack of ammunition and took up position in a shell hole. They held out all day in the hole until they were relieved by the 15th Warwicks on the night of 3 May. The attack had been difficult for many reasons. Due to the artillery barrage one company had not received any rations and continued their assault without being fed. There had been bombing parties under Lieutenant Nilson and Bailey. There were also dugout clearing parties consisting of an NCO and three bombers. A Lewis gunner was supposed to keep the Germans' heads down while the wire was cut. There were few casualties at first, but during the counter-attack the right-hand company lost all of its officers. Nilson was badly wounded and was brought in by Lieutenant Gore.

Another painting by John, which seems to be just landscape, perhaps not anywhere near the front. (C. Chaloner)

Once again, due to the lack of decent communication, some of the battalion were lost during the series of attack and counter-attack. Lieutenant Bull finally got a telephone line to the sunken road where many of the lost men were pinned down, reinstating contact. During the night, Major Winter reconnoitred the whole area while it was under heavy shellfire, proving that not all officers stayed behind the lines in safety.

John tried to connect the effects of the war with a similar event from history. The best example he could think of was the Black Death. He thought the plague and the war were responsible for changing attitudes of mind between the rulers and the ruled. The Black Death had improved the position of the lower classes because after its ravaging effects workers were in short supply. This would be the case after the war. John mentioned a bombing attack on Folkestone and believed that the Germans were mad to attack Britain at this stage of the war and upset the peace cranks. He had little time for those who wanted to end the war and criticised the Archbishop of Canterbury for not supporting British retaliation. He argued that 'when the Hun kill Scarboro's children, we have to offer up Folkestone as well, according to St Davidson'. John seemed to be struggling with some discord between his faith and the war at this time – although anyone who went to war could not be content to simply 'turn the other cheek'. He commented on German religion, wishing that Martin Luther were alive to see what effect such a low-class religion could have on a nation.

Along with the constant movement between short spells at the front and short rest breaks, the 1st Battalion also took part in more training at Noyelles. Large attacks on enemy trenches were not an everyday occurrence, but there were constant small raids by both the British and Germans. The objectives of these raids were usually attempts at taking prisoners, most likely for intelligence purposes. Some of these raids were not so small but became almost full-blown attacks.

During June, there were several honours awarded to members of the 1st Sportsmen. Major Lewis received a DSO, Lieutenant Bull an MC and the regimental sergeant major a DCM. There were nine further Military Medals awarded to other ranks.

Chessire asked in one of his letters if his wife had heard the big explosion in Flanders. They did not hear it where he was stationed, but it all depended on the wind direction. He also told her that the general was wounded and that France retaliated against the Germans by attacking them for their raid on London. He said that the Germans, on hearing about the *Strand Magazine*, bombed the Strand in London. He suspected that they were misled over their intelligence and believed that the Germans thought the magazine was an ammunition dump, not a publication.

In early July, the 1st Battalion was in the Cambrian sector when a raid took place by the Germans. They wounded one man and took another prisoner. When coming under fire, they abandoned their prisoner, leaving him in the trench. The Germans were driven out by bombing parties.

On 20 July, the battalion took part in a raid with 100 men. There was more to this raid than the normal objective of taking prisoners for information: this raid aimed to take the enemy trench. With most of the Germans pulled back, their trenches were barely manned. The few who were there must have put up a fight, as there were two men killed and fifteen wounded in the raiding party.

There has been much written about how the wives of working-class men struggled financially with their husbands serving overseas. There has been less written about those of a higher class whose finances also suffered. The income of John's wife fell drastically because of her father's death. It was left to John's aunt to pay off their overdraft. This was something that John's wife, Dorothy, was not happy about. John wrote of a big push, but seemed to have received little information about it and asked his wife if she had heard anything. It seems that those at home were better informed than those actively participating in the war. He mentioned that the *Paris Daily Mail* was very reticent, including someone named Beach Thomas, whose opinion the newspaper seemed to rely on.

In one of his letters John discussed the difference between the risks run by soldiers and sailors, arguing that the casualties lists showed which service had to put up with the worst dangers and pointing out that sailors carry out their duties under much more pleasant conditions. Surely, he said, the sky and water were much better than mud and lice. John also made an interesting comparison between those soldiers who work in offices and those who are grooms and batmen. He said that there is only one level of intelligence in the Army, and that is a dead one.

By September, the 1st Battalion was at Givenchy. The previous month, the 251st Tunnelling Company blew up the last underground mine of the war in the area. While in the Cambrin sector at the end of the month, several patrols were sent out. A report in *The Times* of 20 September mentioned the bravery of a certain royal fusilier company. The correspondent did not reveal the exact unit or area of this occurrence, so it is impossible to say that it was the Sportsmen, but certain clues point to that possibility. The report stated that a certain unit of royal fusiliers were under heavy artillery fire with hardly any shelter, apart from a collapsed and battered trench. The Germans knew their exact position and the fire was as heavy as any troops could handle. Then through explosions the men began to sing an Army version of a well-known song, *In These Hard Times*, this version far closer to the knuckle than the real one. They sang while crouched in bloodstained water, caring for the wounded and tending to their dead.

The next evening, the correspondent watched the same unit perform a concert in a large canvas marquee at the rear. An audience of around

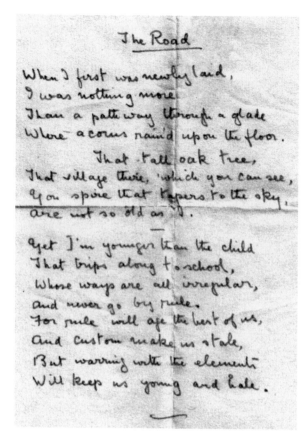

The Road

When I first was newly laid,
I was nothing more
Than a pathway through a glade
Where acorns rain'd upon the floor.
          That tall oak tree,
That village there, which you can see,
You spire that tapers to the sky,
Are not so old as I.

          —

Yet I'm younger than the child
That trips along to school,
Whose ways are all irregular,
And never go by rule.
For rule will age the best of us,
And custom make us stale,
But warring with the elements
Will keep us young and hale.

Left: *By this stage in the war, John Chessire seemed to be running out of news to write to his wife about. So he sent her this poem.* (C. Chaloner)

Opposite: *As the end of the war approached, John Chessire found time for many more paintings and drawings; this is a view of his suggestions for Chepstow Docks.* (C. Chaloner)

500 listened and joined in the rendition of the same song, this time sung by a member of the unit who was a well-known man in London's music halls.

John finally managed to get leave and went home in October, which must have come as a culture shock. He returned to France in November and spent some time at Ostrohove Rest Camp, where the battalion had been based on their arrival in France two years before. He said that then the camp was tents and snow; now it was mainly huts with about 500 men in each.

There were strong rumours in November that the battalion was to be sent to Italy but, as with most rumours, this information turned out to be false. Instead, they were moved to Cambrai to cover for the troops who had taken part in a major attack at the end of October. This had been against concrete pillboxes through deep mud and had not been successful.

Private R.M. Tinkler joined the 2nd Battalion at the age of seventeen in 1916. In October, he was sent to visit a wounded member of the battalion. The two men had been runners together and the other man had been badly hurt in a bombing raid. Tinkler was pleased to find that the doctors thought that the man would live and would soon be on his way back to England. While visiting his wounded friend, Tinkler was given a shopping list for the mess. He mentioned in a letter that a parcel was taken during a raid on an enemy trench that came from Bavaria and contained white sugar and white bread, which suggests that such items were normally unavailable.

There were six attacks by the Germans on the Bourlon-Moeuvres Ridge during November, all of which were beaten off by the 2nd Division. This included the Sportsmen's Battalion who held the line with the rest of the division; then followed two days of constant fighting, when they were finally forced to withdraw. During this time they killed large numbers of the enemy and held off an attack that could have had serious consequences if it had been successful. Some actions of the British were victorious and included the capture of part of the Hindenberg Line. There followed a series of triumphant attacks and counter-attacks, by both German and British troops.

The Sportsmen were intended to take part in an assault but were instead moved to Bourlon Wood where the Germans were counter-attacking. A British charge captured the wood but were almost wiped out by German artillery. Nonetheless, there was several successful raids during November. It was reported in *The Times* that London troops staged one raid that led to the death of 100 Germans and the taking of fourteen prisoners, along with the capture of four machine-guns and two trench mortars.

By December, the Germans had more luck and part of the British line fell, causing the rest of the British troops, including the Sportsmen's Battalion, to fall back. During this time two sections of A, B and C Companies were left as rearguard as the battalion fell back to Hermies. There was an example of the battalion's quality of men that month, involving Second Lieutenant Hugh Bird. Bird came from Stanmore, in Middlesex, and after attending the Central Foundation School in London he became a clerk for the London & North West Railway Company at Euston. He joined the Queen Victoria Rifles at the outbreak of war and rose to the rank of sergeant before being commissioned into the 1st Sportsmen's Battalion in May. He had been in France since June, and in December he had been in command of an important post when he and his men managed to kill a German machine-gun crew and capture the gun. He was awarded the Military Cross for his actions. Also in December, Lance Sergeant Cochrane and Private Hemington volunteered to deal with a derelict tank which was being used as cover by German snipers. They crept out to the tank under heavy fire and threw two mills bombs into the hulk, killing the snipers. They returned safely amid heavy machine-gun fire.

Christmas was spent in tents at Gropi Camp while the battalion was in reserve. Although this may have seemed a pleasant end to the year, heavy snow did not make it a comfortable one.

CHAPTER 11

1918

January was spent in divisional rest, and in February the battalion moved to Equancourt as reserve. By 9 February, they moved again to Vacquerie and went back into the line.

John Chessire began the year with a thesis on the eating habits of the working class. He felt that if the working classes had a more educated palate they would not always want the same dishes at the same time. He believed that everyone should have to dine out once a week in an establishment where nothing was served as mother would make it. Eating out would have been beyond the means of working-class men but if this occurred to John he did not let on. 'Staple foods vulgarise the mind', he maintained. He deplored the suet pudding the troops were served, which was deadening in its effect and brought everyone down to the same level.

John was worried about one of his children, Dodo, who seemed to suffer heart problems. He suggested that she be kept home from school for a term and spend her time drawing. Several of John's opinions indicate a domestic mentality and lifestyle that was rather simpler than today, although of course this was no longer applicable to life in the trenches.

Thoughts of the end of war were circulating amongst the troops. Lectures were held on what would happen after the war. John was well versed about events occurring at home, such as Birmingham beating Manchester in the collection of war bonds for tanks. There were new docks at Chepstow and John believed that they should widen the Severn Canal.

John did not lose his sense of humour. He accused one of his children of being unpatriotic for catching German measles and described the illness as a poor imitation of Britain's own measles. By the end of February, the war had reached a dull but critical stage. John said that the Old Moores Almanac stated that the world would end in AD 3187, pointing out that they would need to get a move on with the war otherwise the ends of the world and the war would clash. The Sportsmen had spent much of the previous two months moving from one sector to another. They had spent a lot of this time in reserve, until going back into the trenches in February.

March led to the battalion's move to the hutted camp in Metz but, despite the comfort of staying in buildings for the first time in many months, the camp had been shelled which did not help the men to relax. In the middle of March, the battalion was back on the line and suffered from heavy gas attacks. Lieutenant Colonel Winter lost his voice during this period, along with many of the battalion, because of the heavy gas shelling of Highland Ridge. When they were relieved, most of the men were suffering from the effects of the gas. While they were in reserve, the Germans launched a major attack, firing artillery on the battalion's camp. The battalion was turned out to stop the enemy from breaking through and was successful in holding them at Beaumont Hamel, the site of the final Battle of the Somme. The next day the enemy attack was beaten back.

This was the beginning of the great German offensive, which was to be their last attempt at winning the war. On a front of more than fifty miles, half a million Germans attacked. The British 3rd Army held, but the 5th Army was forced to withdraw. More Germans were sent into the fray and began to make several gains. At one point, the Germans advanced forty miles in a week, a distance unheard of in previous years of the war. The 1st Battalion was successful in holding their part of the line against the initial German waves, but the troops either side of them fell back. This left the Sportsmen in a dangerous position and they were forced to fall back to avoid getting cut off.

Reports in newspapers at home on 4 March mentioned a German attack on the French and Portuguese lines. The attacks were described as a number of disconnected local activities, rather than any grand operation. There was no hint of what was to come for those at home. On 9 March, there was a report of an attack by the Germans on the British, near Ypres. The Germans used flamethrowers and some of the

Two small cards that John sent from France. (C. Chaloner)

advanced British posts were forced back. There was a distinct increase in restlessness along the whole front line, as large German offensives were reported in the press as gaining nothing.

Reports of the war on the Western Front suddenly became quite scarce in British newspapers. There was a great deal of newspaper interest in air battles and air raids, while reports of any attacks by either side were not mentioned. It is not certain that this was a deliberate attempt not to report the German attacks but it does seem strange that the Western Front was hardly mentioned during this period.

It was not until 22 March that news of a great German attack appeared in the press, which had taken place the previous day. It was along a fifty-mile front, the largest of the war so far. There were reported to be large German losses but there was as yet no mention of British casualties. The attack had been preceded by heavy artillery bombardment, but the British did not have any deep shelters to retire into as the Germans did on the Somme. Moreover, many of the German troops were experienced in war and were previously on the Eastern Front, unlike the new recruits the British had during the attack on the Somme. Many parts of the British front were destroyed and the Germans made great advances, but some British troops survived and put up strong resistance, holding up the attack. It was then reported in the press that some progress had been made by the enemy and that parts of the line had been forced back to their reserve trenches. There was a clear attempt by the media to break the bad news to the public gently. Field Marshall Haig made a statement that the men were fighting with great gallantry and that this was especially true of the 24th, 3rd and the 51st Divisions.

By 25 March, reports admitted that the British had, in many cases, retreated to the line previously held before the Somme. There was a sign that something was going seriously wrong when the Lord Mayor of London sent Field Marshall Haig a telegram stating that the city of London had full assurance in their British troops. A notice appeared in *The Times*, written by Rudyard Kipling, reading, 'We are fighting for our lives and the lives of every man, woman and child, here and everywhere else'. It was suggested that the notice be pinned to the reader's desk or mantelshelf so that they would not forget its words. The notice went on to describe what would result from a German victory and its wider meaning for the population.

Private W.A. Hoyle, of the 2nd Sportsmen's Battalion, wrote a detailed record of the retreat before the German attack, until he was wounded and went back to England. He gave the handwritten report to a nurse at the VAD hospital in Cranbrook, Kent, where he was treated. The record is now in the Imperial War Museum in the papers of H. Russell, the nurse's husband.

The 2nd Battalion was on the front line on 20 March and due to be relieved. Hoyle reported that there was a lot of activity by German aircraft, as well as heavy shell and mortar fire. The battalion was taken off the line that night by an officer who had nothing to carry on his back. He tried to hurry the men, exhausted after their front line duty, and loaded down with equipment. They arrived at a light railway and loaded aboard the trains. Shortly after leaving the area, it became the site of a heavy German barrage. Although worn-out when they finally reached their huts, they were told to get into fighting order. There was five days' worth of mail waiting for them but they had to read it while being shelled. They had to be ready to fight, sleeping with their clothes on.

On 22 March, the battalion was supplied with extra ammunition and bombs. At 4.00 a.m. they marched through Haplincourt and arrived at a dry canal that had huts built in the bottom of it. After spending the night in the huts, they were told to destroy them the following morning. They then fell back to some old trenches, which they had to get into better order and support a division in front of them. However, the men

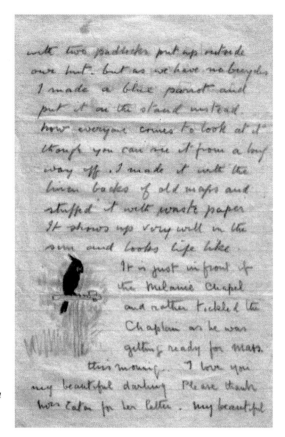

Another letter from John with a small drawing of a parrot.
(C. Chaloner)

in front of them fell back, leaving the 2nd Battalion as the front line. All that day British artillery guns were passing the Sportsmen's lines on their way back to the rear. When even the light guns went past them, they felt as if they had been left on their own. A party was sent out that night to the battalion headquarters. When they got there they were attacked by the Germans. They held a line by the railway while headquarters was evacuated. The battalion then moved back to another trench and were told to hold it. A patrol went out and captured a German machine-gun, sneaking round the back of it and killing the crew.

By 24 March, they were on the move again, this time backwards. Hoyle said that everyone was moving back. Tanks were sent out in front of the retreating troops but either broke down or were put out of action by the Germans. The battalion was almost surrounded again and again and continuously fell back. By this time, half of the battalion was missing.

On 25 March, the confusion amongst the British became clear to Hoyle and the rest of the 2nd Battalion. They were on the road to Miramount again, ready to move back, when they were told to hold their position at all costs. They held out until lunchtime and again fell back. A captain stopped them and told them to return to their lines. Then a colonel appeared and said that the lines were held by the Germans, so they had to fall back.

The battalion on 26 March was at Beaumont Hamel and some of the missing men had turned up to swell their numbers. There was a quarter-mile gap in the lines on their left and no one available to fill it. They were shot at from behind and were unsure if they had been surrounded or if the Germans now held Beaumont Hamel.

A man showed up dressed in a French officer's uniform and turned out to be German. He was shot as a spy and some men wearing British coats began to try and encourage the battalion to move towards them. These men turned out to be Germans as well and they were also shot.

They were nearly out of ammunition when some men arrived with more. The men made several trips to replenish supplies, just in time for the battalion to beat off another German assault. During the attack, Hoyle was hit in the hand by a bullet from a German machine-gun. He said that it felt as if he had been hit on the hand by a hammer. By this time, no one knew who, or what, was behind them, so Hoyle decided to go back and find out, making his way down a communication trench. At one point Hoyle had to climb out of the blocked trench and was shot at. He then was nearly bayoneted by an Englishman who would not let him pass because an officer refused to believe that Hoyle was English, not knowing that anyone else was in front of them. It was only when a man in the ranks recognised Hoyle that he was allowed through and sent back to a first-aid post. He spent the night in a Canadian hospital, and by 29 March he was back in Dover.

During March, Lieutenant Bird, of the 1st Battalion, was given leave and returned home. While there, he received the Military Cross, awarded to him in the previous December, from the king at Buckingham Palace. He then returned to France. In fact, 88,000 men on leave in Britain were recalled at that time because of the German advance. Bird became involved in what was part of an amazing series of events upon his return to duty. On 25 March, while he was fighting a fierce rearguard battle, Bird was killed by a shell. This happened while rallying his men to meet a German attack. A telegram was sent to his wife on 5 April informing her of his death. Lieutenant Colonel Winter also wrote to Mrs Bird, saying that her husband had been a gallant officer of great promise. There was a memorial service for Bird held at the Stanmore Church on 20 April. His death was reported in the *London & North Western Railway Gazette*. The final sentence of the report said that since the story had been written, news was received by the War Office giving reasonable hope that Lieutenant Bird was not dead, but rather a prisoner of war. It sounds an incredible story but it is in fact what had happened. One can only wonder at the emotions of his wife who became a widow and then found herself reinstated to marriage within a few weeks.

John Chessire must have been speaking of this German attack when he said in one of his March letters that the outlook of the war was more hopeful than it seemed. John was evidently looking for positives in a very bleak situation. There were even rumours of leave being granted but this was cancelled within days, no doubt following the German successes. He said that the dry weather was too beneficial to the Huns but could not imagine that at this stage in the war they could go dancing on ground that had taken so much to reclaim. John had not seen a newspaper for several days, so his wife at home in England was likely to have been more aware of the position than he was.

One aspect of the conflict that was often overlooked was the position of civilians in war zones. They were moved out when the Germans first invaded but some returned to their homes when the Germans were pushed back and began to build their lives again. With the German's new offensive, some of these civilians faced the prospect of losing their homes all over again. Moreover, there was a danger of losing more than their homes: shelling behind the lines often caught civilians and led to many fatalities.

The 1st Battalion took up position on the front line but were soon forced back again. They were finally pushed back as far as White City trenches, where they held the enemy until the New Zealanders relieved them. Colonel Winter took command of the brigade during their next spell at the front, due to the death of Brigadier General Barnett-Barker; Major Lewis took command of the Sportsmen's Battalion. Lewis was taken prisoner and command was taken over by Captain Bowyer until Winter returned, after a new commander was appointed to the brigade. During March, the battalion suffered over 200 casualties from gas and more than 200 from wounds taken in the fighting after the gas attacks. March was a good month for the Germans, who achieved some very good advances. The British lost 38,000 men, of which 21,000 became prisoners of war. This did not benefit the Germans, who had to feed them while short of supplies for their own troops. Many of the most advanced units of the enemy had out run their supply lines and were receiving no rations.

The news seemed to be better for John by the end of the month. He wrote of how pleased his wife must be to read how well the British Army was now doing since the big fight began. Ever patriotic, he said the Hun had made a mistake in throwing his weight against the British and that the German attacks and successes of the fortnight had some advantages in re-awakening the public's interest in the war.

By April, John was certain that the Germans were desperate to end the war that year. He believed that it would be possible to capitalise on their desperation and looked for hopeful signs for the Allies in the German successes. He said that the war was now moving so fast after its previous slow pace that it was hard to follow from day to day. The Germans were not pleased with their gains when they were weighed against the expense of keeping them. John explained that the *Morning Post* did not seem favourably impressed with the steps Lloyd George had taken to deal with the Hun offensive. It appears he was more concerned with his popularity than with the British Army being cut to pieces.

April continued to be just as successful for the German attack. Their advance did not seem to be running out of steam, although the Allies were beginning to hold them in some places and even counter-attack in many areas. On 11 April, the order of the day from Field Marshal Haig stated every position should be held to the last man. He went on to say that 'with our backs against the wall the safety of our own homes and the freedom of mankind depend on the conduct of each one of us.' He had been influenced by the words of Kipling. It was the first time that many of the men had been told that there was a chance that they may lose the war. This stark comment held special significance when spoken by such an esteemed member of the high command.

John was on the move again by the end of the month. It was the fourth move in three weeks, so the German offensive was having some effect on him. He told his wife that he was back at the place from which he had started from two years before. Once again he was suffering his two pet peeves: rats and shelling. However, the vibrations of the shells did scare the rats away. John had a new man in his office, an architect who designed Westminster Town Hall and other famous buildings. Before his arrival, he was working fatigue duties.

The 1st Battalion spent much of April on and off the front line in several different areas. By the beginning of May, they were moved back to billets at Berles au Bois for training. Some of this involved bayonet training, which seems a bit strange during this time of the war. The battalion strength during the month was as follows:

1st May	Strength	Officers	36	Other ranks	861
	Killed		1		0
	Wounded		1		22
	Sick		0		52
	Commissioned		0		2
	Struck Off		4		19
	Reinforcements		4		49
31st May	Strength		34		815

There was heavy rain at the beginning of May, which John felt was a pity for the men in the trenches. In dry weather, the water was often 3ft deep in the trenches and was even worse in the rain. Some people took a gloomy view of the ground lost to the Germans. John once again looked for the good points in the German advance: they had moved so far that their lines were stretched and not as well defended. Gas drills were practised because of expectations of the Germans using gas to attack rear areas. With further gains, May was just as successful for the German advance. At one point it looked as though they might reach Paris. John's attempts to look on the bright side began to appear misguided.

Even so, late in the war the Sportsmen's habit of resolve and a positive outlook had not deserted John Chessire. He mentioned that the Huns seemed to be in no mood to make the next move but supposed that it might come any day. He also said that they would never get the pitch in better order. It was in May that John was transferred to the 272nd Employment Company. This happened because so many units broke up or were absorbed, so that many men were left with no units at all. He did not know at that time if the Sportsmen's Battalion still existed. In 1918, brigades were reduced from four to three battalions.

The war was linked with sport again at the end of May, when John asked his wife what she thought of the German innings. They seemed to think more of making runs quickly than in keeping up their wickets, he pointed out. He noted that Costa Rica had declared war on Germany. He did not take this seriously, saying how many of the Empire's forces were still available to be tapped, like the Egyptian Crocodiles holding the line in marshy areas, or the Giraffes as observers and the Whales for mine sweeping.

There were some interesting comments about German sporting activities in a book written by J.W. Gerard, the previous American ambassador to Berlin, called *Face to Face with Kaiserism*. He described sport in Germany as consisting of shooting, hunting and racing, but these pursuits were reserved for nobility. Even foxes were shot, an activity that would have horrified the fox-hunting fraternity of England and reinforced their distrust in the sporting character of the enemy. The rifles Germans used for hunting were mainly Mauser rifles, with adaptations of telescopic sites. Not adverse to a little hypocrisy after complaining about the British view of war as sport, the Duke of Ratibor collected as many of these rifles as he could and sent them to the front to be used by snipers.

The beginning of June saw no improvement to the serious situation for the British. John Chessire wrote that he understood the anger at home over the recent war news. The past four years of action had been a question of using trench warfare, until the British Army was strong enough to advance. It is now difficult to appreciate the difference brought about by the open war, forced upon the Germans in their frantic haste to press for a decision before the Americans could become too effective.

There were several theories at the time speculating why the Germans were suddenly so successful. One idea put forward by the *Daily Mail* was that Germany had a better understanding of likely weather conditions and so had timed their attacks to coincide with three months of dry weather. British attacks always seemed to occur during wet spells causing them to struggle through deep mud.

By June, however, there were more Americans arriving at the front, which was beginning to make a difference. Towards the end of June, John Chessire described the new influenza, which lasted about two or three days, making you feel very sorry for yourself. He called it 'fashionable', something which the many thousands who died from it at home would not have agreed with. In his next letter, he named it as the Spanish Flu and said that it affected most people in the head. It took until early July for John to take the illness seriously, when many men had temperatures of 104°F. The illness prevented him from competing in a sports day, which must have been a serious irritation for a Sportsman. By the end of June, the 1st Battalion was back at the front and A Company took part in a raid on the German trenches, with B Company following. The German attacks were beginning to fail by July. Spanish Flu may have had a similarly damaging effect on the German troops.

John was given leave to go to Paris in July and told his wife that there were numerous air raids. The war was now going better for the Allies, which John attributed to the Hun's suffering from Spanish Flu in higher numbers than the British. He asked his wife if it was true that an officer's train was mobbed at Victoria. John was very pleased to be recognised by Colonel Hudson, who crossed the street to shake hands with him while in Paris. He had recognised John as a member of the Sportsmen's Battalion. The colonel said that he would have asked John to lunch with him if that had been possible, which suggests that colonels could not lunch with privates, even if they came from the same class.

In Juy a battalion member was killed. Harry Prior had joined the Sportsmen in the summer of 1915 and fought in several battles, until he left to return to England in January 1917. Harry joined a cadet corps at Trinity College, Oxford, and received a commission in July. He was then attached to the Royal Flying Corps. He was taking part in training in a new aircraft when it went out of control and crashed, killing him instantly.

Once again, the battalion returned to short spells of rest and front line action. That continued until August, when they took part in the attack with the 3rd Army. The battalion went over the top at Ayette and captured Aerodrome trench. Others then passed them to capture Courcelles, where they all finally stopped for a rest. During the same month, Thomas Peck joined the battalion. Peck had been working in munitions, so did not have to enlist but decided to do so with three of his friends. Although they all joined up together, they ended up in different regiments. Peck was sent to Hounslow to the Royal Fusiliers, where he was given his uniform before being sent to Ireland for training. Peck said that the fourteen weeks' training was a wonderful experience. This training included drilling, bayonet practice and firing. He spent some time in Dublin and Belfast before being given two-weeks' leave after completing training. He was surprised to learn that their instruction did not include going over the top of the trenches, as he had seen this happen in newsreels at the cinema.

After a few days in France Peck moved to the Cambrian Sector, to the right of the Somme. The newcomers travelled in cattle trucks on the railway. The men he was with were mainly Londoners and seemed to treat the whole experience of going to war as a joke. Peck said he did not feel scared and that he had been trained well enough to deal with what he had to do. After arriving in France, Peck's first experience of battle was to cross No Man's Land in artillery formation with groups of six men – attacking in lines was now less popular. Most of the casualties suffered by the battalion were from the British artillery barrage. When they reached the enemy trench, there were only three Germans. One was killed by a Lewis gunner by mistake and the other two were standing around smoking cigars. One experience that Peck described as frightening occurred when they were in a trench in the dark. They often had to step over men who could have been either asleep or dead. There were tin cans hanging on the wire to warn of attacks, and during the night the cans began to rattle but it turned out to be a rat.

Getting into the trenches was a problem in itself. The men always moved up at night and travelled in pitch blackness. They walked on wooden duckboards led by a white tape that showed them the way. Peck was never sure who was actually at the front leading, perhaps an officer. They would arrive at the communication trench, which made finding the way easier. They usually went up to the front line once or twice a week. By the time Peck arrived in France the Germans were on the retreat, so there were no large attacks. Once in the trenches, they either just sat there or went out into No Man's Land to take up forward positions. They would usually spend about an hour on the firing step before someone else took over. If they wanted to look over the top they used periscopes, but most of the time they just sat around doing nothing. They might be told that they were to go on a raid the night before it happened, but were never told why. Knowing that they were going out on an attack was worrying, but Peck always felt confident that he would not get killed.

Some nights they would be sent out in small groups, usually six to a group, to take up forward positions. Once they went out without even

1918

A painting of a peaceful winter scene. The winter of 1918 was to be more peaceful than the previous ones.
(C. Chaloner)

their corporal to tell them what to do, as he had been wounded. Peck suggested that they should have a sleep that night, while two of them took turns to stay awake. The rest of the men took offence at his trying to tell them what to do and ignored him, but they all fell asleep. Their luck ran out and they were caught by the sergeant who said he had a good mind to shoot them all.

Peck said that the German trenches were far superior to the British ones. They were usually deeper and better dug. One reason given for this was that the Germans were more defensive-minded than the Allies, who were expecting to be attacking more, so did not need to concentrate on building such well-fortified trenches. The only problem with using captured German trenches was that the dugouts would be facing toward the enemy – not that Peck experienced much in the way of attacks. There was some sporadic shellfire and machine-gun fire from the enemy but that was all at this stage of the conflict. Peck was 'number three' on a Lewis Gun, which meant that he carried eight very

191

heavy poniards, as well as his own equipment. He would keep the ammunition poniards clean with a shaving brush. His own equipment included a rifle, bayonet, trenching tool, a gas mask and a water bottle, from which they were not allowed to drink without orders.

When Peck reached the Hindenberg Line, he found a number of British dead hanging on the wire in a dried-out canal. There was a wounded German who they thought was dead but he began to fire on them as they passed. The officer with them shot him dead with his revolver.

Peck lost all his mates over time. He said that men usually palled up with about six mates, although you knew all the others in your unit. When all your close mates died, you had to make new friends. Peck was eventually hit by a sniper's bullet that went through one man then hit him in what he thought was his foot. He managed to get himself into a sunken road where another man cut off his trousers to find the wound, which turned out to be in his thigh. He remembered being annoyed because he had just been given new trousers. Although stretcher-bearers found Peck, they had no stretcher and so had to help him hobble back. Loss of blood made Peck feel faint and they had to stop until some men from a trench used a blanket to carry him back to the First Aid Post.

What happened next was a blur to Peck. He woke up in a large marquee after an operation. The small hole in his leg was now an enormous cut and the bullet that had been in there was by his bed. The wound had turned out to be a blighty one. Most of his journey home was a haze, as he was kept in a drugged state. He ended up in a hospital in Birmingham. He spent some time in the hospital, where he remembered the doctors being quite brutal. There were no crutches available, only a walking stick. While in the hospital his brother was due to be married, so he asked for special leave. He knew he would not get it for a wedding, so he told them he needed it on domestic grounds. It turned out that taking leave counted as a discharge from the hospital. Despite being wounded, he was sent to guard German prisoners in Huntingdon. His job was to march the prisoners to work with farmers in their fields but his wound meant he could not keep up with them, so he went sick.

The beginning of September saw an attack by the 1st Battalion on Slag Avenue. They suffered over 100 casualties. The advance continued and the battalion supported the capture of Noyelles. John Chessire mentioned the success on the Western Front and cheerfully remarked that it would soon be time for the Germans to find out how much a return ticket to Germany cost. Although John often commented that the Germans were short of rations, he sympathised with his wife over the shortage of writing paper at home, while telling her that they could get plenty of writing paper off German prisoners. He went on to say that education classes were being set up for the soldiers in France and he was considering applying for a lecturer's post. He also said in one of his letters that a young boy from the Royal Artillery would soon contact his wife. He heard the boy was going on leave to Cheltenham and asked him to pass on a message to Dorothy as to how he was.

At the end of September, the 1st Battalion was ordered to send out strong patrols to gain the river and canal crossings at Noyelles. There was an artillery barrage, which was supposed to move before the advancing men. Unfortunately, the barrage fell between some of the advancing companies and the headquarters, cutting off communication. Consequently, there was surprise amongst the Germans when Lieutenant Anderson and his platoon reached Marcoing. The two German gun crews, who were attaching the guns to their limbers, were not expecting an attack until after the barrage passed. Anderson shot the crew of one gun and captured it, but the other group escaped with their gun.

There was only slight opposition in most areas, and Lewis Guns were set up to protect bridges over the canal. Two other platoons reached Noyells and took several prisoners, who were still in their pyjamas. They found some parts of the canal were better defended than others. The Germans knew by this time that they were defeated and at the end of September Ludendorff and Hindenberg told the Kaiser that the war was lost. Under Wilhelm II the military became the highest social ranking in the country, but now they had let him down.

In early October, the battalion were attacked at Forenville by infantry and enemy tanks; they found the Germans still had some fight left in them. The battalion held on to their position. During this attack, Lieutenant Anderson and his batmen went off the line to challenge a German tank. They hammered on the side and called on the crew to surrender. The door opened and the crew climbed out and were taken back as prisoners.

John mentioned that Turkey had surrendered early in October and that he doubted if Austria would carry on much longer: Germany would not carry on alone. He also wrote of how little of France now remained in enemy hands. By the end of the month, there was news from home that the Spanish Flu epidemic had become very serious, and in many cases fatal.

After another spell in reserve, the battalion moved back up to St Python. They attacked and captured Ruesnes. This was the last action seen by the battalion, as it moved back into reserve on 26 October.

John Chessire had a period of leave at home at the end of the month and found it much harder to return to France, as he dreaded the journey back. The trip through England was fine. He even enjoyed two hours of freedom in Folkestone before crossing the Channel. Once in Boulogne, he was put up ten to a tent, with only a thin blanket for each man to keep out a heavy frost. The train to take him back left at 7.00 a.m. the next day and did not reach the railhead until the next morning at six. Then it was off on a 40km walk.

Once back in France, John noted that the civilians were returning to the area in which he was based. There was, however, nowhere for them to live and nothing in the shops for them to buy. He believed that the Germans never took the French Army seriously, except at Verdun, and that it was the British who bore the brunt of all the heavy fighting.

The Armistice was signed and the war ended at eleven on 11 November. The troops were ordered to stand fast wherever they were but not to have any interaction with the enemy at this time. While church bells rang in England and celebrations began, a telegram arrived at the home of poet Wilfred Owen's parents, informing them of his death.

In a later despatch from Field Marshal Douglas Haig, he described the events of the end of the war and the advance into Germany. Initially, troops were ordered not to advance and German prisoners were to be freed. The allied positions were to remain in place allowing the Germans to withdraw. There was to be a 10km gap between the retreating Germans and the advancing Allies, who began the march into Germany in November but were not to cross the border until December. This would involve the 2nd and 4th Armies. The advance was described as being of the highest military order. The troops were welcomed by the local population as they travelled through what had previously been occupied Belgium. Large numbers of allied prisoners were also appearing at regular intervals during the march, having been released by the Germans; which development further stretched the Allies' already meagre supplies.

In front of the Hindenburg Line. November, 1918

Parts of the Hindenberg Line had been breached, as these ruins of the German defences show.

Many of the bridges across the Rhine had been destroyed and some were still mined and often exploded, causing supply problems. There were more shortages now that the war was over, due to the difficulties in travelling with supplies. There was to be a sad ending to the war for a number of the battalion's men: after surviving through the trials of conflict for so long, six members of the Sportsmen died of influenza during November 1918.

By the end of November, John wrote about the lectures on demobilization, which were well received by the troops. He recognised a problem that would beset the economy at home with so many casual labourers being released from the forces at the same time. It was not only labourers who were about to find it difficult to get work. Advertisements began to appear in *The Times* from ex-officers who were seeking employment.

John saw the king, who travelled through their village, looking better than he had when John last saw him in London. In Germany, the royal family was not having such a good time. Willhelm II abdicated when he was told that the German Army could no longer be relied upon. The German Navy was also heading towards open rebellion. A republic was declared in Germany in November and there was competition between various political groups for supremacy. The king came back again a few days later and this time stayed a little longer. There were rumours that the troops based in England were being allowed leave and finding jobs, which gave them a great advantage over those men still in France. Meanwhile in France, John described his surroundings as consisting of empty factories and aimless troops now that the fighting was over.

By Christmas, John reported that those who went on leave and found a job did not have to come back. This caused yet more resentment amongst those still stuck in France.

The end of the war led to a relaxation in duty for the battalion. The men spent the rest of the year getting back into shape. The end of the war meant a return to the Bull cleaning and polishing of pre-war days. The actual interval between the end of the war and the demobbing of the troops had the potential to be the most trying time of the whole conflict. In one camp, Kimmel Military Camp, in Canada, there was a long delay in freeing the men from the Army. The result was a meeting followed by a riot in which twelve men died, including a major.

The British fell back on a tried and trusted plan to occupy the men. The Army Sports Control Board believed that, deprived of an outlet

The Sportsmen found themselves in Cologne. This is the theatre in the city.

for energy, the men could find that discipline became relaxed and fall into mischief. A solution to this concern was considered to be the promotion of sporting competitions and games between units. The competing units were to be the battalion.

The Sportsmen's Battalion undertook the 200-mile march into Germany, looking like soldiers again, to join the more than 30,000 men who were to garrison part of Germany. The Allies were not the only troops to march into Germany. The German armies themselves marched home in good order and were received as heroes and victors, rather than losers.

In the beginning of December the German 6th Army entered Cologne. The whole city was bedecked with flags, and there was a triumphal arch hung with the old imperial colours for the troops to march beneath. A banner said that the German River and the German Cathedral greeted the hero bands. Cigarettes and flowers were handed out to the troops by the crowds who greeted them. However, there was no cheering from the troops, who marched in silence. Unlike the British troops, they did not wait around for demobilisation. They simply went home.

The occupation of a nineteen-mile bridgehead across the Rhine began when the British cavalry crossed the Hohenzollern Bridge on

12 December. The bridge was flanked by bronze statues of past German emperors. The cavalry was observed by generals Plummer and Jacobs as they crossed the river. When the armoured cars crossed there were no men visible, so they dipped their guns when passing the saluting point. The area the British were to occupy stretched twelve miles along the river and nineteen miles inland. The infantry was to follow the cavalry and cross the river the following day.

When the infantry began to cross the bridge the next day, General Plummer was watching them in the rain. Each battalion was led by its own band: the Sportsmen marched across the bridge to the tune of *The British Grenadiers*. When the British Army arrived in Cologne, including the detachment of armoured cars, German civilians flocked out to see them. Lieutenant General Charles Ferguson took up his post at the Hotel Monopol and the Union Jack was raised above the hotel. A general order was issued that interaction with the local population was to be confined to the essentials, conducted with courtesy and restraint. The occupation of the area around Cologne was completed without incident. When *The Times* correspondent arrived to inspect the cavalry posts a few days after they arrived, he said that it seemed as though they had been there for weeks. They were going about their work with complete ease, as though they had been doing it for some time.

The locals seemed to accept the prescence of what had until recently been enemy troops. However, although they seemed unconcerned, the correspondent noted that at times you could see a trace of hatred in their eyes. Half the population seemed curious, the other half indifferent. The German children would often cheer the British troops as they travelled through the streets.

Although the German Army had been short of supplies at the end of the war, in Solingen there was plenty of food. Shop windows were full of luxuries, despite rations having been reduced. Solingen was a rich production area during the war. In restaurants, the helpings of food were large, which at first the correspondent suspected was due to the British uniform, but then noticed that civilians received the same portions.

There was to be little Christmas cheer for the British Army from home. The sending of parcels to those troops still abroad was prohibited because of the strain it would put on the transport system. The public was told not to send Christmas puddings or other perishables, as the troops would be given puddings.

An army camp in occupied Germany. Each tent was for two men.

There was some sad news for the Sportsmen's Battalion at the end of the year. The obituary column in *The Times* of 27 December mentioned the death of Mr Edward Cunliffe Owen CMG, of 26 Leicester Road, Loughborough, after a long illness. Edward was the husband of Emma Cunliffe Owen, who had been responsible for raising the battalion, and the only child of the late Colonel Henry Cunliffe Owen, of the Royal Engineers, and the late Mrs Willington. The funeral took place at Kensal Green Cemetery on 31 December, and Edward was buried in the family grave. Unusually for a relative of the Royal family, he had been accepted into the Roman Catholic Church shortly before his death.

CHAPTER 12

1919–20

The previous year, before the end of the war, a fourteen-point plan for peace had been put forward by American President Woodrow Wilson. The plan was intended to obtain 'peace without victory'. The Paris Peace Conference was held in January and was attended by the thirty-two nations who had played a part in the conflict. The main decisions were made by the 'big four' of Britain, France, Italy and the United States. Wilson's 'fourteen points' were largely ignored during the conference. The European powers had suffered a great deal more than America in the conflict and wanted Germany to pay.

Although the war was over and the release of men from the Army was underway, there were ongoing issues to address. It was not only in Germany that troops were still prevented from returning home. It seems that disbanding the Army was as problematic as recruiting. John Chessire wrote that he still had a lot of work to do on the maps. He mentioned how unstable things were in Germany, with so many groups trying to gain an upper hand. He also spoke about how the Bolsheviks in China were trying to take control of the country. He said he doubted that this would happen, although perhaps this was wishful thinking on his part. The end of the war marked the beginning of new dilemmas for the world. John went on to talk about the war casualties. As the French lines were four times longer than the British, proportionally the number of casualties proved that it was the British who did most of the heavy fighting. He criticised the low French birth rate, which led to a shortage of French soldiers.

John sent a poem relating to release from the Army:

Left: *The American occupation forces were given copies of this history of the Rhine by the YMCA. It is unclear whether the British received anything similar.*

Opposite: *Mounted British soldiers on the streets of occupied Germany.*

Folkestone Town

The mayor was smiling at the troops.
Smiling with all his might.
He did his very best to keep the happy warriors bright.
And that was difficult because there was no leave in site.

The general and his adjutant were walking hand in hand.
They wept like anything to see so many out of hand.
If these were all demobilised they said it would be grand.

If seven clerks on seven machines typed forms for half a year.
Do you suppose the general said that this would get us clear.
I doubt it said the adjutant and shed a little tear.

If seven ships with seven slips sailed daily from Bolounge.
Before we reached the pivotals we'd all be forty-one.
Quite likely said the adjutant and groaned another groan.

Let seven educationalists teach all the troops to swim.
I think you might with safety then demobilise the slim.
And those without their papers-well dismiss them with a hymn.

Douglas Haig wrote that the men who were stationed in Germany might have been thinking about going home but they realised the need for a force to be stationed in Germany. Because of this understanding, and the innate courtesy of the British soldier, examples of misbehaviour had so far been very rare.

Nonetheless, there were to be no chances taken. A new military department was used for the first time in occupied Germany. The Special Investigations Branch was a plain-clothes detective branch of the military police – although when on duty in foreign countries they often wore uniforms.

Sir Eric Geddes had been placed in charge of the demobilisation of forces. There were several meetings to discuss the matter, meetings which included Douglas Haig and Winston Churchill. The target was to release 50,000 men a day, but Churchill believed that this would leave the British Army of the Rhine (BAOR) very short of men. He maintained that the Army in Germany should realise that they could not be released until the fruits of victory had been gathered. Churchill's idea was that the Army should by now consist of men who were late joining in the war – last in, last out. The exception to this were men who had been employed in important jobs before enlisting.

During a dinner at the Mansion House in London, with the lord mayor, Churchill appealed to employers to keep keep jobs open for those men who had been kept in the Army. Churchill went on to explain that 900,000 men were needed for the defence of Britain and its Allies' interests. The plan was to let three out of four men leave the Army, while paying the fourth double to stay and finish the job.

The eventual plan was to turn the Army back into the volunteer force that it had been before the war, which proved equal to the tasks given to it. Churchill reported that over 1,000 men were volunteering for military service every week but that training them would take time. Meanwhile, they needed trustworthy persons to be left on the Rhine to look after the interests of Britain.

John mentioned that the education scheme for the troops who were about to be demobbed was opposed by the trade unions. By the end of the month, John was himself about to enter the demobilisation machine, which was supposed to take six days to complete. He did not have much faith in this timescale but it must have been successful, as this was the last letter he sent.

The beginning of the first year of peace found the Sportsmen's Battalion at Niederaussem in billets as part of the British Army of Occupation, which became known as BAOR. They were still training and there was a revival of the battalion's interest in sport. Several football matches and paper chases were arranged for them. The pattern of activity for the BAOR was training in the morning, with organised recreation (sport) in the afternoons and whist drives in the evening. Voluntary education classes were offered to the men.

Although the military postal system had been working well during the war, tests were carried out in 1918 using specially adapted aircraft to carry military mail. These tests, organised under the Royal Engineers, worked well and this was to be the world's first airmail service. It operated between Folkestone and Cologne to carry post to the BAOR.

One of the swimming medals awarded to the winning competitors during the sports competitions of the British Army of the Rhine (BAOR). There is a Royal Fusiliers emblem on the back.

At the end of January, the King's Colour was presented to the battalion in Germany by Major-General Pereira. He praised the battalion for its magnificent service, comparable to any other battalion in the Army. It was a tribute to the British race that a newly formed battalion with no previous traditions could outfight German battalions trained to war for years. The Sportsmen left the 99th Brigade and travelled by train through Cologne to Ehreshoven and joined the London Division before taking over the occupied zone at Lindlar in March.

On leaving the 99th Brigade, the Commander Brigadier General McNamara said that he had high appreciation for the oldest members of the brigade and their magnificent service while part in it. The battalion had taken a leading part in the many battles of the brigade. The battalion had shown great discipline and spirit, which had eventually beaten down all resistance.

The situation in Germany was far from stable at the time. The streets around the government offices in the Hotel Eden were barricaded with barbed wire, machine-guns and artillery. The situation was close to civil war when the government made a positive move by arresting Dr Meyer, the well-known Sparticist leader. Several factors in Germany were combining to cause political problems. The government had most of the population behind it. The Berlin Workmen and Soldiers Council were supported by the Socialist workmen of Berlin. Kurt Eisner, in Munich, had control of Bavaria and was in favour of a separatist policy. Then there was the Army, which was in favour of the government.

Rioting and looting were rife in many cities, including Cologne. Appeals were launched for the British Army to come into the area early to assist in controlling these outbreaks. The cavalry and machine-gun units had been sent in advance. When they reached Cologne, they were initially on one side of the river separating the city and British sentries would walk halfway across the bridge to meet German sentries. Meanwhile, there were still cases of rioting on the German side, although suspicion grew that this was mainly perpetrated by hooligans, rather than those with political motives. The political situation caused spiralling inflation and the British Army was now being paid in marks. However, as it was impossible for shopkeepers to increase prices in line with the falling value of the mark, British troops were financially doing quite well.

At the end of March, the blue grenades were removed from the badge of the Sportsmen's Battalion. In the battalion diary, this was reported as being 'abolished by a higher authority'.

In April, the battalion absorbed the 52nd Battalion Royal Fusiliers, which brought its strength up to forty-three officers and 756 other ranks. They were sent back to Cologne and command was taken over by Lieutenant Colonel L. Ashburner. The commander of the BAOR, Baron Palmer of Messina and Bilton, left. He was replaced by Sir William Robertson, an ex-teacher who joined the ranks of the Army in 1877. Day tours of the Rhine were organised for the men. On 7 May, the battalion travelled by rail to Overath to take over from the 7th Battalion, of the Middlesex Regiment.

In May, the Allies finally presented their demands to Germany. The Germans had expected to be dealt with under the guidelines of the 'fourteen points' and were shocked at the severity of the demands. They had to pay 132 billion marks. Where this was to come from was not explained and the country was as good as destitute. The amount was finally toned down to 37 billion marks in 1930. What the Allies achieved from this was of far less significance than the negative effect on the feelings of the German people.

Germany was also to lose its overseas colonies. It lost Alsace Lorraine to France. Poland was again brought back as an independent country and given parts of Prussia. Germany lost other territory in Europe too: the Western Rhineland was to be occupied by Allied troops for fifteen years, while the German army was reduced to 100,000, and there was to be no German airforce.

It was possible that there would have been further fighting in June if Germany had refused to accept the peace treaty. It looked for a time as if Germany would refute the harsh terms the Allies were intent on imposing. The Sportsmen's Battalion was ready to march further into Germany if needed. In the event the Treaty of Versailles was only signed by Germany after threats by the Allies to fully invade the country from the already occupied areas. However, orders for an advance were cancelled after the treaty was signed.

Back in England, some members of the battalion were bidding each other goodbye. Thomas Peck was finally invalided out because of his wound in July. He was given a medical discharge with £1 per week pension. He had several medicals, wherein it was revealed that he now had one leg shorter than the other. Peck said that if he had lost a bit of his finger, or been disfigured, he would have received a pension for life. Despite no longer being able to play sports, Peck was given a lump sum of £40 as final payment.

Much of the battalion's time in Germany in those last days, after the threat of further fighting declined, was spent engaging in sport. They won most of the prizes at a brigade swimming gala in June and lost only in the final of the Kalk football cup.

The British European Forces (BEF) Sports Board had come into existence a few months before. The patron was the Prince of Wales and the objective of the board was to improve the fitness of the BEF troops. The plan was to encourage the men to compete for the honour of the unit, playing for the team rather than for themselves. To encourage proper sporting etiquette there were to be no more monetary prizes. However, there would be souvenirs, of no real value, for winners of individual events and trophies for team sport winners that would be held by the unit. This termination of cash prizes was not strictly adhered to. In August, there was a race at Cologne Racecourse for the BAOR. The participants came from several cavalry units and the Royal Horse Artillery, which were based in Germany. Prize money for the winners was 3,000 marks. The Sportsmen were not only successful in sport, as they also topped the list of the VI Corps for war savings in July.

Meanwhile, the numerous war graves on the continent were in the process of having their wooden crosses replaced by stones. It was possible for relatives of the dead to be sent the crosses from their loved ones if they wished. They simply had to write to the War Graves Commission in London to receive them.

By 1920 the situation in Germany had not yet settled down. In March, a French soldier was shot dead by the citizen guard. They accused him of being a poacher. There was an attack on Allied officers by German soldiers in a camp in Brandenburg. While supervising the demobilisation of the remaining members of the German Army, a French, Belgian and British officer were shown around the camp by a German officer. The inmates began jeering them and threw stones at them, injuring the Belgian. Yet by no means were all interactions between the Germans and Allies violent: in Sheffield, a German girl from Cologne was taken to court, after following a sergeant from the Royal Engineers across borders without a passport, before reaching England. It seemed that the sergeant, despite being married, had helped the girl by giving her money. There were calls to expel the girl.

There was a revolution reported in Germany on 15 March. The government in Berlin was overthrown by a party led by Dr Wolfgang Kapp. There was a deal struck between the new chancellor and the old one, who had fled, to hold an election within months. This turned out to be false and fighting broke out in Berlin within days, including the use of machine-guns. Within days, it was Kapp who had fled and the old government was reinstated, but the fighting did not stop. Certain groups, such as the Socialists, wanted to take advantage of the unrest. Meanwhile, the Allies, who formed the occupation force, seemed largely unconcerned with the upheaval. It was only the French

A menu for a farewell meal before the battalion returned to England.
(C. Chaloner)

who held serious misgivings about the situation. Many believed that it did not much matter which party ruled Germany and preferred to stay out of the argument.

The end came for the Sportsmen's Battalion in March 1920 when they finally disbanded. This decision seems untimely, considering the unrest in Germany at the time, but evidently there were few real worries about the political situation in the conquered country. The Sportsmen's Battalion had survived with a longer life than any other service battalion of the Royal Fusiliers.

CHAPTER 13

AFTER THE WAR

Viscount Maitland presided over about 250 previous members of the Sportsmen at the Great Eastern Hotel. Unfortunately, the newspaper clip reporting this information was not dated, but it must have been released some time around 1920 as a detachment from the battalion, stationed in Germany, was present.

Also present were Colonel H.A. Vernon DSO, who had succeeded Viscount Maitland in command, and Lieutenant Colonel E.A. Winter DSO, the third commander of the battalion. Others present included Major Lewis, Major Jourdain, Captain Bull, A. Barr, F. Charlier, A. Clark, L. Colman, P. Essex, W. Fry, P. Geach and G. Roberts.

Viscount Maitland toasted absent comrades, as well as the 23rd Royal Fusiliers. He mentioned that one special thing that had struck him was the way the battalion fought at Deville Wood. Lieutenant Colonel Vernon replied that the battalion would do anything and go anywhere that was humanly possible. Winter mentioned the wonderful spirit which animated the men right through the days when, with no equipment but nice white gloves, they marched through London and did not even give eyes to the guards.

From the original battalion, over 500 men went on to become officers in other regiments. When they went to France, there were thirty-one officers and just over 1,000 men. Total reinforcements numbered 188 officers and 3,752 men. The casualty list read:

	Officers	Other ranks
Killed in action	26	427
Died of wounds	2	128
Wounded	81	2,216
Missing	19	831
Total	128	3,102

Although many of the Sportsmen survived the war, not all of them could return to their sport. Ernest Hayes was a cricketer and before the war had played for Surrey. He made one appearance in a test match against Australia and also played some games for England against South Africa. After the war, he decided to retire due to damaged hands. However, he did go to Leicestershire as a coach and was persuaded to play again at the age of fifty.

After the war, there were several military matters to be resolved. Lieutenant Bird returned home from captivity and was in the Prince of Wales Hospital, in Marleybone, when he received a letter from the War Office asking for the details of his capture. It was later found that no blame should be attached to him. In April 1920 he was informed, while at the Royal Fusiliers Convalescent Hospital for Officers, at Brighton, that a notification would appear in the *London Gazette* on 4 May stating that he would relinquish his commission due to ill health caused by wounds. It was not until 1924 that Bird was examined by the Ministry of Pensions at Chelsea. They found that he was 60 per cent disabled by gunshot wounds in the right thigh and suffered from deafness. He was awarded £126 per annum pension. Bird was not alone in his disability. By the time the Second World War began, more than 100,000 ex-soldiers were receiving pensions for either physical or mental disability caused during the war.

Frank Heath, of the 2nd Battalion, returned to Cornwall having being invalided out of the Army after being gassed. He continued his painting and exhibited at the Royal Academy and Paris Salon. He became known as the 'Sunshine Artist' and a book was written about him entitled *Frank Gasgoinge Heath and his Newlyn School Friends at Lamorna*, by Hugh Bedford. Heath died in 1936.

R.M. Tinkler joined the 2nd Battalion in 1916 at the age of seventeen. He survived the war and went on to join the Shanghi Police force. He became a detective inspector. He was killed in 1939 by Japanese marines who were trying to break up a strike by Chinese workers in a cotton mill where Tinkler was then employed.

Right: *A 1930s advertisement for houses being built on the Grey Towers Estate.*

Below: *Grey Towers Avenue in Hornchurch was built on the site of the driveway leading up to the old house.*

213

The Army no longer had any need for anyone but battalion members and Grey Towers House was empty of troops by June 1919. For a short period, Grey Towers was used as a camp for Brownies and Guides. In 1922, the estate was sold to Mrs Elizabeth Parkes, of Langtons, which reunited it with the original estate after fifty years. In 1929, the 146-acre Langtons Estate, including Grey Towers, was sold to Allen Ansell for £20,000. He sold it on to Grey Towers Estates, a company formed by Ernest and Frederick Legg, who were to develop the site. The land was then sold off in small sections to other developers, who subsequently built houses on them. A number of roads were built, including Grey Towers Avenue, which ran along the site of the old driveway up to the house. Part of the land along the main road is now used as allotments, and the small brook still runs through this area.

Hare Hall is still standing today and is now part of the Royal Liberty School, opened in 1921. The old mansion is the rear part of the school, with more modern buildings at the front. There are some wooden out-buildings there that look suspiciously like the wooden huts in which the soldiers of Hare Hall Camp resided.

Most of the previous grounds became part of a private housing estate. One advantage to the area initiated by the soldiers from Hare Hall was the increase in the number of shops. Once the soldiers left the area, the new custom was maintained by residents of the new houses. Balgores House, as drawn by Frank Heath, still exists and has been through several uses, including a nursery school.

Clipstone Camp, briefly used as a demobilisation centre, closed just after the war. The camp was mainly dismantled, and many of the huts were taken away and used around the area as school classrooms and church halls. Some of the buildings on the site were used for housing those working in the nearby mines. New homes were built on the site. Even the old guardhouse was put to use as a shop for those living on the site, until the 1930s. The area surrounding the camp still has some open spaces and woods and there is evidence of the trenches dug by the men from the camp and part of the old sewage works.

In 1936, there was a reunion dinner for the Sportsmen's Battalion at the Arundel Hotel, on Arundel Street Strand. A letter of invitation was sent out, unfortunately undated, for the 5th Annual Dinner of the Sportsmen's Battalion, presided by Lieutenant Colonel Vernon at the Connaught Rooms, Kingsaway, London. Tickets were 10s each.

BATTALION STRENGTH AND HONOURS

Battalion Strength	Officers	Other Ranks
When leaving for France	31	1,006
Reinforcements received	188	3,762
Total	219	4,762
Casualties		
Killed in Action	26	427
Died of Wounds	2	127
Wounded	81	2,216
Missing	19	331
Died of Illness	0	11
Honours		
DSO	5	
Bar to DSO	1	
Military Cross	27	
Bar to MC	5	
Order de l'Caronne	1	
DCM	14	
Military Medal	93	
MSM	8	
French Croix de Guerre	1	
Belgium Croix de Guerre	1	
Italian Bronze Medal	1	

APPENDIX 2

SOME OF THE MEN AND THEIR CAREERS

Bates, W.E., Private	Yorkshire county cricketer
Butler, The Hon. B.D., Private	son of Lord Lanesborough, ex-champion golfer of Sussex and member of the MCC
Cambell, Rae Brown, Private	author
Canton, C.F., Corporal	big game hunter
Cooper, P.H., Sergeant	clergyman
Cumming, Sergeant Major	champion walker of Britain
Curle, J.H., Private	mining engineer and author
Delany, J., Private	lightweight boxing champion of England
Dillion, C., Private	comedian, a dame in many pantomimes
Freer, C.C., Private	journalist for the *Daily Mail* and second editor of the *Sportsman's Gazette*.
Harrison, J., Private	middleweight boxing champion 1912. and member of Grenadier Guards until 1910
Holmes, S., Captain	son of Colonel Holmes, owner of Grey Towers
Noyes, R.T., Sergeant	all-round sportsman and member of the expedition to relieve Gordon at Khartoum
Stackpole, R. De Vere, Lieutenant	cousin of novelist and previous member of Dragoon Guards
Vincer, E.S., Private	marine engineer and only Englishman to have killed a bull in a Spanish bullring
Warner, D.R., Private	cousin of General Sir Douglas Haig, marksman and golfer
Wharton, A., Corporal	comedian
Williams, J.J., Private	conjurer, journalist and psychology lecturer

APPENDIX 3

DEATHS (NOT FROM WOUNDS)

Although the vast majority of deaths amongst the Sportsmen were due to enemy action, there were other fatalities, notably from the outbreak of Spanish Flu that hit the battalion hard after the war ended.

Name	Date	Cause of death
Richards, E.W., Lance Corporal	18-10-16	self-inflicted wound to the head
Bull, W.J., Private	24-3-17	kidney tumour
Olding, J.L., Lance Corporal	21-4-17	collapsed dugout
Dooley, D., Private	29-4-17	falling from a railway carriage
Bennet, C.R., Private	8-1-18	pneumonia
Mansbridge, R., Private	17-1-18	heart failure
Watts, G., Private	23-1-17	accident (no details)
Reeves, H.D., Private	3-7-18	pleurisy
Wood, W.L., Lance Corperal	1-11-18	influenza
Hall, F.P., Private	15-11-18	influenza
Colley, T.N., Private	18-11-18	influenza
Petty, T.S., Private	18-11-18	influenza
Pickles, J.H., Private	18-11-18	influenza
Spright, C., Private	19-11-18	influenza

The plaque commemorating the Sportsmen's Battalion was placed in St Andrew's Church in Hornchurch after the war, the church in which the men had worshipped during their time at Grey Towers.

BIBLIOGRAPHY

Banks, T. & Chell R., *With the 10th Essex in France* (Burt & Sons, 1921)

Benton, T., *The Changing Face of Hornchurch* (Sutton, 2001)

Carr, William, *A Time to Leave the Ploughshares* (Robert Hale, 1985)

Cowper, *The Task* (1785)

Croman, D., *A History of Tidworth and Tedworth House* (Phillimore, 1991)

Daily Mail (5 November 1914)

Essex Countryside (April 1975)

Essex Record Office Document (D/DS 206/121)

Essex Times (17 October 1914)

Essex Times (14 November 1914)

Essex Times (26 June 1915)

Essex Times (17 July 1915)

Essex Times (7 August 1915)

Evans, B., *Hornchurch and Upminster* (Phillimore, 1990)

Fareham, J.C., *Clipstone Camp* (Privately Published)

Foley, M., *Frontline Essex* (Sutton, 2005)

Georgem David Lloyd, *War Memoirs of David Lloyd George 1915-16* (Little Brown, 1933)

Great War Magazine (9 January 1915)

Great War Magazine (20 April 1918)

Hastings, M., *Warriors* (Harper Collins, 2005)

Imperial War Museum, Account of Battle of Somme (ID 4797)

Imperial War Museum, Correspondence of Formation of Sportsmen's Battalion (ID 71836)

Imperial War Museum, Interview Thomas Peck (ID 9365)

Imperial War Museum, Private Papers, Lieutenant Bird (ID 1004)

Imperial War Museum, Private Papers, Major Wolff (ID 4797)

Imperial War Museum, Heath F G (95/16/1)

Imperial War Museum, Stephenson (04/38/1)

Imperial War Museum, Ferrie Captain W.S. (03/19/1)

Imperial War Museum, Ferrie Captain W.S. (03/19/1)

Imperial War Museum, Worger S.R. (84/15/1)

Imperial War Museum, Tinkler R.M. (P8)

Imperial War Museum, Russell H. (76/119/1)

Laffin, John, *Tommy Atkins* (Sutton, 2004)

Mannox, B., *Hornchurch and the New Zealand Connection* (Havering Library, 1993)

Mansfield Chronicle (1 July 1915)

Marples, Pauline, *Forest Town, The Village that Grew Out Of Coal* (Forest Heritage Group, 2005)

Morning Post (5 November 1914)

National Archives, Document WO (Battalion Diaries, 95/1372)

Newnes Illustrated (5 June 1915)

O'Neill, H. C., *Royal Fusiliers in the Great War* (Naval & Military Press Ltd, 2002).

Parker, Peter, *The Old Lie* (Constable, 1987)

Perfect, Charles, *Hornchurch During The Great War* (Benham, 1920)

Perfect, Charles, *Our Village* (Perfect. 1912)

Reed, Douglas, *Insanity Fair* (1938)

Romford Times (20 January 1915)

Romford Times (2 February 1915)

Romford Times (10 February 1915)

Romford Times (12 October 1915)

Sassoon, Siegfried, *Memoirs of a Foxhunting Man* (Folio Society, 1971)

Sassoon, Siegfried, *Memoirs of an Infantry Officer* (Faber & Faber, 1922)

Sketch (7 November 1914)

Smith, R., *Hornchurch Scramble* (Grub Street, 2000)

Standard (10 November 1914)

St Ives Weekly Summary (21 September 1916)

The Times (28 August 1914)

The Times (7 September 1914)

Thomas, Edward, *Selected Letters* (Clarendon Press, 1996)

Wardm F., *The 23rd Service Battalion Royal Fusiliers, First Sportsmen* (Sidgwick & Jackson Ltd, 1920)

Waterford News (18 February 1916)

INDEX

If you are interested in purchasing other books published by Tempus,
or in case you have difficulty finding any Tempus books in your local bookshop,
you can also place orders directly through our website

www.tempus-publishing.com